Law, Climate Emergency and the Australian Megafires

This book addresses the ways in which the Black Summer megafires influenced the development of climate narratives throughout 2020. It analyses the global pandemic, and its ensuing restrictions, as a countervailing force in the production of such narratives.

Lives and properties were lost in the spring and summer of 2019 and 2020, when catastrophic bushfires burnt through millions of hectares of mainland Australia. Nearly 3 billion native animals died. And for millions of Australians, and others worldwide, it was through the Australian megafires that the global climate emergency became tangible and concrete, no longer a comfortably deferred, albeit problematic abstraction which could be consigned to future generations to deal with. This book explores the legal and other implications of new understandings of climate emergency arising from the fires, and the emergence of a hierarchy of emergencies as the pandemic came to dominate global and domestic political discourses. It examines narratives of culpability, and legal avenues for seeking retribution from government and big fossil fuel emitters. It also considers the impact of the fires on the burgeoning phenomenon of climate activism, particularly in Australia, and the ways in which pandemic restrictions curtailed such activism. Finally, the book reflects on the fires through the lenses offered by climate fiction, and apocalyptic fiction more generally, in order to consider how these shape, and might shape, our responses to them.

This important and timely book will appeal to environmental lawyers and socio-legal theorists; as well as other scholars and activists with interests in climate change and its impact. It is recommended for anyone concerned about current and future climate disasters, and the shortcomings in legal, political and popular responses to the climate crisis.

Nicole Rogers is based in the School of Law and Justice, Southern Cross University.

Photograph by Martin Von Stoll

Law, Climate Emergency and the Australian Megafires

Nicole Rogers

Routledge
Taylor & Francis Group
a GlassHouse Book

First published 2022
by Routledge
2 Park Square, Milton Park, Abingdon, Oxon OX14 4RN

and by Routledge
605 Third Avenue, New York, NY 10158

a GlassHouse book

Routledge is an imprint of the Taylor & Francis Group, an informa business

British Library Cataloguing-in-Publication Data
A catalogue record for this book is available from the British Library

Library of Congress Cataloging-in-Publication Data
A catalog record for this book has been requested

ISBN: 978-0-367-62356-2 (hbk)
ISBN: 978-1-032-11703-4 (pbk)
ISBN: 978-1-003-22116-6 (ebk)

DOI: 10.4324/b22677

Typeset in Times New Roman
by Apex CoVantage, LLC

This book is dedicated, with gratitude, to the memory of two remarkable women:

Annette Coyle (1951–2009), friend, activist and much-loved godmother to my daughters; and Margit Maria Fekete (1908–1998), who risked everything to hide my father and grandmother during the Holocaust.

Contents

Acknowledgements

I am very grateful to my family, including my parents, my daughters Freya and Lillika, and my husband Brendan, for their support and encouragement. Two people in particular contributed to the writing of this book: Professor William MacNeil minimised my teaching commitments during a challenging year to provide me with time and space, and Colin Perrin from Routledge suggested the project and facilitated its development. I would also like to acknowledge the bravery and commitment of Greg Rolles, Emma Dorge, Holly Porter, Clancey Maher, Tom Cotter and all the other climate activists prepared to argue the extraordinary emergency defence in the relatively hostile environment of Queensland courtrooms. Many thanks to all the wonderful people who have assisted them with this, including Sue Higginson, Jacquie Svenson and Benedict Coyne.

1 Black Summer and all that followed

Nicole Rogers

In the spring and summer of 2019 and 2020, catastrophic bushfires burnt through millions of hectares of mainland Australia. These would be referred to, subsequently, as the megafires, and the period during which the fires raged is known as Black Summer.

Some prominent members of the federal government argued against any links between the bushfires and climate change, with the Deputy Prime Minister at the outset adopting an openly derisory tone towards the 'pure, enlightened and woke capital-city greenies' who drew such a connection.[1] Yet, as the megafires took hold throughout Black Summer, other federal and State politicians conceded that climate change was a causal factor.[2] In early December 2019, Prime Minister Scott Morrison, a staunch supporter of Australia's mining industry, notably acknowledged that climate change was playing a contributory role.[3] In October 2020, the New South Wales Transport Minister, who had been forced to shelter on the beach with other fire refugees during Black Summer, identified climate change as the predominant cause of the 'fire tsunami'.[4]

On the first day of hearings of the 2020 Royal Commission into National Natural Disaster Arrangements (hereinafter the Natural Disasters Royal Commission), established to investigate the Black Summer bushfires and, more generally, Australia's capacity to respond to future natural disasters, the central focus was on the interconnection between the megafires and climate change. Witnesses addressed the changing global climate, and consequential risks. Karl Braganza, Head of Climate Monitoring in the federal government's own statutory agency, the Bureau of Meteorology, explained the mechanisms by which climate change was 'load[ing] the dice' towards worse fire seasons,[5] with longer seasons, an increased frequency of large-scale heatwaves, and more extreme fire danger days.[6]

The three Commissioners were left in no doubt that climate change was already causing 'extreme weather and climate systems that influence natural hazards', and that locked-in global warming over the next two decades

DOI: 10.4324/b22677-1

will lead to rising sea levels, more intense tropical cyclones, and more frequent and intense floods and bushfires.[7] They stated, in their Report, that catastrophic and unpredictable fire conditions, such as those experienced during Black Summer, will become more common in Australia.[8] The causal contribution of climate change to the megafires was also recognised in the report of the 2020 New South Wales Bushfire Inquiry.[9]

The science was undeniable. A group of scientists reached the conservative conclusion that at least some of the drivers 'show[ed] an imprint of anthropogenic climate change'.[10] After assessing available, peer-reviewed, scientific publications, the authors of a 2020 Bushfires Project report acknowledged the causal link between a changing climate and worsening fire weather conditions, such as those experienced during Black Summer.[11] According to another group of scientific researchers, 'scientific assessments that human-caused climate warming is virtually certain to increase the duration, frequency and intensity of forest fires in southeast Australia' were borne out during Black Summer.[12]

For Australians of all political persuasions, including 'quiet Australians',[13] the connection between climate change and the megafires was clear. During Black Summer, Liberal politicians were reportedly 'bombarded' with emails from 'mainstream mums' concerned about the government's climate inaction.[14] According to the authors of the Australia Institute's 2020 *Climate of the Nation* report, published at the end of October, an increasing number of Australians believe that they are currently experiencing climate impacts;[15] bushfires were the 'climate change impact of concern' for 82% of Australians surveyed several months after Black Summer finished.[16] There was a demonstrable correlation between direct experience of the fires and climate change concerns.[17]

A group of 80 Australian Research Council Laureate Fellows wrote in an open letter in January 2020 that '[t]he tragedy of this summer's bushfires' had made it clear that '[c]limate change has arrived, and without significant action greater impacts on Australia are inevitable'.[18] What, then, did this realisation mean for climate narratives in Australia: narratives at work in the political arena, in courtrooms, on the streets and through other forms of activism, and in fiction?

Black Summer

In the spring and summer of 2019 and 2020, as catastrophic fire danger ratings occurred at locations and times never yet recorded[19] and temperature records were broken, fires raged through an estimated 19.4 million hectares[20] of mainland Australia. Some of this was World Heritage listed, with over 80% of the Blue Mountains World Heritage area and over 50% of the Gondwana World Heritage area impacted.[21]

Bushfires are commonplace in Australia, and a number of devastating fires have already occurred this century. These include the 2003 fires in Canberra, the Black Saturday fires in Victoria in 2009, which led to the deaths of 173 people, and the 2013 Red October bushfires in New South Wales. Yet the megafires were extraordinary by any measure: in duration, in magnitude and in sheer destructiveness. They burned through areas previously thought to be too wet to burn.[22] They generated an exceptional number of pyrocumulonimbus events: fire-caused storms considered to be very rare.[23] The Gospers Mountain fire, which began on 26 October 2019 and burned until February 2020, was, at that point, the largest recorded forest fire in Australia[24] and, reportedly, Australia's first 'mega-blaze'.[25]

The scale and impact of the fires is almost impossible to comprehend; this is symptomatic of what Timothy Clark has called the scalar framing of the Anthropocene.[26] Millions of Australians saw the fires, felt their heat, witnessed their destructive force and inhaled their smoke throughout that never-ending summer. The fires impressed themselves, strongly and irrefutably, upon 'the given dimensionality of our embodied existence'.[27]

Yet the fires were also a 'planetary environmental reali[ty]'.[28] Satellite images depicted an enormous, ominous expanse of smoke and fire; one year later, John Kerry, newly appointed climate envoy to the Biden administration, stated that these images 'ought to stop every single one of us in our tracks'.[29] One extraordinary aspect to the bushfires was the fact that the smoke travelled so far, allegedly circled the globe.[30] The fire-generated pyrocumulonimbus storms pushed a huge smoke plume 35 kilometres into the stratosphere; this vortex persisted for 13 weeks and travelled 66,000 kilometres.[31] One of the researchers who documented the unprecedented phenomenon described it as 'jaw-dropping'.[32] Smoke from the fires was still detectable by satellite a year later.[33]

The megafires brought devastating loss of human and nonhuman life, and property destruction. The impacts and after-effects of the fires, both short-term and long-term, transcend these immediate losses.

Impacts of the megafires

There is no Australian precedent for destruction of such extraordinary magnitude in such a short timeframe, although the effects of the colonisation process are comparable. In fact, the fires augmented the destruction wreaked by colonisation, with estimates of thousands of Indigenous cultural sites lost to the flames.[34]

Australian wildlife and biodiversity were dealt a profound and potentially irreversible blow. A wildlife carer observed that 'there is a scent of death in every breath'[35] and, similarly, Douglas Kahn described the communal inhalation of 'hectares of endangerment'.[36] Scientists have estimated that 327 threatened species had a 'significant portion . . . of their known distribution within the fire footprint'; 114 species lost at least half of their habitat, and 49 species experienced the destruction of over 80% of their habitat.[37] Animals that survived the blazes had to find food and avoid predators in a 'moonscape landscape',[38] and the magnitude of the destruction impeded resettlement by impacted populations.[39]

Again, the scale of the disaster is difficult to comprehend. According to a scientific report commissioned by the World Wide Fund for Nature, nearly 3 billion native vertebrates,[40] including over 60,000 koalas,[41] were killed or displaced by the fires: a figure far exceeding the initial estimate of 1 billion animals. The Fund's Chief Executive has described the fires as 'one of the worst wildlife disasters in modern history'.[42]

Human survivors – those who lost their homes, were trapped for hours and days on beaches, in lakes, in cars on blocked roads, and in evacuation centres, fought the fires as volunteers, heard the agonised screaming of trapped koalas in the burning trees, returned to charred properties in the aftermath to contend with dead animals, smouldering ruins and blackened landscapes – will be suffering from psychological trauma and mental health impacts for a long time. Children in particular are vulnerable to long-term, mental health impacts.[43] For many, particularly the uninsured, the financial consequences were calamitous.

The insidious health impacts are as yet unknown. Millions of people who were not immediately endangered by the fires endured a summer of endless, toxic smoke. Canberra-based climate scientist Sophie Lewis wrote that '[t]he smoke's persistence, heaviness, health impacts and power to evoke panic couldn't be adequately articulated'.[44] Social researchers estimate that approximately 11.2 million adults, or over half of the population of Australia, were physically affected by this,[45] with medical researchers finding that the smoke caused 417 deaths and a total of 3151 hospitalisations.[46] Given the impact of the fires on catchment areas, there was, furthermore, a very real threat of contaminated water supplies affecting large numbers of people.[47]

The fires, themselves climate-charged, exacerbated global warming by creating a huge upsurge in Australia's carbon emissions.[48]

The ripple effects extend beyond these. For Australian people, there has been an all-pervasive and, for many, brand new realisation of our terrible vulnerability to climate impacts. There is the tarnishing of our international image, with an Austrade report finding that Australia's reputation as supplier of goods and travel destination suffered during Black Summer.[49] This was, in part, due to 'perceived ineffective disaster management practices and inaction on climate change'.[50] There is 'collective grief' for past, safer summers, as if they were 'a lost idyll'.[51] There are the beginnings of mass movements, both voluntary and enforced, away from bushfire-affected or fire prone areas, and the first acknowledged wave of Australian climate refugees.[52]

The climate emergency became tangible, no longer a comfortably deferred, albeit problematic abstraction. Climate change was now a visceral experience for millions of Australians; it had been seen, breathed, tasted and felt. Award-winning filmmaker Lynette Wallworth, speaking at the World Economic Forum in Davos in January 2020, described herself as 'a traveller from a new reality: a burning Australia', in which '[w]e have seen the unfolding wings of climate change'.[53] The fires were, in the words of climate scientist Joëlle Gergis, 'a terrifying preview of a future that no longer feels impossibly far away'.[54]

Although Australia's vulnerability to climate impacts has long been recognised, it has been a truism in climate discourse that those who contribute least to climate change are in the frontline of climate impacts. This point has been repeatedly emphasised by the small island States, described by the Fijian Prime Minister as 'innocent bystanders in the greatest act of folly in any age'.[55] Robert Aisi, representing Papua New Guinea, stated in the United Nations General Assembly in 2007 that '[w]e are likely to become the victims of a phenomenon to which we have contributed very little and of which we can do very little to halt'.[56]

Thus, the advent of Black Summer highlighted a significant global anomaly. As journalist David Wallace-Wells put it, Australia is 'the one exception to the cruel rule of global warming and global inequality'.[57] There have been other First World climate crises: Hurricane Katrina, Hurricane Sandy and the 2018 Californian wildfires spring to mind. Later in 2020, wildfires of similarly unprecedented scale and intensity raged relentlessly through the West Coast of the United States, with one of the fires, the August complex fire, designated the world's first 'gigafire'.[58] The Australian megafires themselves occurred in the context of a prolonged, horrific drought, and followed fires in Tasmania's ancient forests and mass fish kills in the Murray-Darling river system earlier in 2019. It was, nevertheless, a rude awakening for Australia to experience the devastation and disruption of a climate crisis of this magnitude, and to be scrambling for the resources to respond. It is a notable irony that neighbouring, less wealthy nations, with their own heightened climate vulnerabilities,[59] generously sent financial and other forms of assistance to Australia during the crisis.

Inevitably, the obstructionist, complacent approach taken by the current Australian government and previous governments to climate action became the subject of intense debate and criticism against the backdrop of the climate-charged fires. There was growing awareness and condemnation of Australia's role as climate spoiler, to adopt Judith Brett's term.[60] Australia's leading role in producing and exporting coal, and its Energy Minister's intransigence at the 2019 Madrid COP25 in relation to carryover carbon credits, were widely deplored.[61] In late 2020, Christiana Figueres, one of the main architects of the *Paris Agreement*,[62] described Australia's internal climate wars as a 'suicidal situation';[63] a view also promulgated by novelist Richard Flanagan.[64]

Pandemic

Much initial commentary, during the megafires and in their immediate aftermath, was focused on their transformative possibilities.[65] Novelist Thomas Keneally suggested that perhaps these fires would 'germinate an essential concept' in similar fashion to the germination by fire of so much Australian flora.[66] In Kim Stanley Robinson's 2020 novel *The Ministry for the Future*, a lethal heatwave, which kills 20 million people, triggers dramatic changes in India; the nation becomes a global leader in climate action,[67] determined 'to change whatever needs changing'.[68] Many hoped that the fires might create such a radical shift in Australia's political culture and climate policies. Yet, at the same time as the megafires decimated vast areas and undid our culturally entrenched assumptions about the sanctity of the Australian summer, another threat was looming. In December, the Chinese city of Wuhan became the epicentre for what would, by March 2020, develop into a global pandemic.

The pandemic reconfigured political, social and economic life in Australia and elsewhere in the world. It heralded a 'double disaster' for bushfire victims, who had lost their homes and relocated to sheds, tents and trailers; they found their difficult circumstances compounded by the challenges of social isolation and enhanced hygiene requirements.[69] Businesses in fire-affected areas struggled to survive. As the pandemic raged throughout the world and came to dominate *all* discourses, the megafires faded into the background and existing climate narratives were paused, and even derailed.

Sophie Cunningham found herself, when writing about the bushfires, 'pulling and tugging at the fabric of [the work] to incorporate the devastating impact of this pandemic'.[70] The same could be said about my own writing process as events unfolded. My starting point in this project was the question of whether and, if so how, the megafires would contribute to the development of climate narratives throughout 2020. As the work progressed, it became clear that the pandemic could not be disregarded in any such analysis. In looking at the evolution of climate narratives throughout 2020, I have considered the impact, and interplay, of two extraordinary phenomena, both 'imbued with an atavistic, biblical solemnity':[71] the megafires and the pandemic.

Pandemic and megafires: points of intersection

Commonalities between these phenomena are apparent in causal factors such as ecosystem and habitat destruction, prior and largely unheeded warnings by experts, the ill-preparedness of both governments and the public, and sheer destructiveness on an unprecedented scale. The virus, as a zoonotic disease, is intimately connected to the climate crisis and, as Andreas Malm has suggested, represents a manifestation of a 'secular trend' of 'global sickening' in the same way that the megafires constitute a manifestation of the parallel, secular trend of 'global heating'.[72] More zoonotic diseases, and more megafires, are inevitable developments in a rapidly warming world.

In the initial phase of the pandemic, graphs depicting the exponential growth in diagnosed cases of COVID-19 evoked the familiar, hockey stick curve of rising greenhouse gas emissions; both were a portent for global catastrophe. The timescale for each phenomenon was, however, quite different. The climate crisis is dire and urgent, but the graphs of rising emissions date back decades. COVID-19, despite prior pandemics, despite the appearance of earlier coronaviruses in the twenty-first century, despite the proliferation of scientific and medical warnings, descended suddenly upon the world 'as an instantaneous and total saturation of everything'.[73]

Mobility restrictions featured strongly during both emergencies, as did masks. 2020 was a year in which the commonplace act of breathing became a fraught and hazardous activity. Photographic artist Aletheia Casey observed that danger, initially in the form of smoke and later taking on the aspect of a terrifying new pathogen, 'lurk[ed] in the very air'.[74] Novelist Jennifer Mills pointed out that the possibility of spreading disease through one's own exhalations created 'a moral entanglement'.[75] The vulnerable and afflicted struggled with every breath. In May 2020, black American George Floyd died at the hands of a police officer in Minneapolis, while gasping 'I can't breathe'; his words, widely reproduced on banners and masks in the Black Lives Matter protests that followed, had a broader resonance.

During Black Summer, Australians found themselves in a state of hypervigilance, of heightened awareness to danger, as they monitored the news coverage of the fires, scrutinised daily air quality readings, and consulted apps and Rural Fire Service maps in order to gauge the proximity of fires. Doomscrolling continued into the pandemic, with different but equally compelling triggers. There was no safe place. The megafires made it clear that our homes, even those in urban areas, do not necessarily offer refuge. Similarly, as Kate Galloway has noted, the first pandemic lockdown revealed 'the limits on the concept of home as sanctuary'.[76] Jilly Boyce Kay observed that, for many, the home 'represents precarity, violence and terror'.[77]

The two phenomena, and their proximity in time, led to widespread discussion of a 'new normal':[78] a resigned acceptance of catastrophe, and the accompanying discourse of emergency, as commonplace rather than rare occurrences. Jennifer Mills, creator of fictional climate dystopia, noted that she had transitioned within the space of only a few months from 'writing about Australia's bushfires while standing knee-deep in the floodwaters in

Venice' to reflecting on the 'numberless days' of pandemic lockdown in Italy; she speculated that '[m]aybe the world is like this now, a series of rolling emergencies without enough time between to measure meaning'.[79]

The problematic interplay between climate hazards and pandemic public health measures was almost immediately apparent to researchers, who warned of the need to manage compound risks.[80] Had, in fact, the pandemic and the Australian megafires occurred simultaneously, the economic and social impacts would have been far more serious; for instance, the potential for disease transmission in crowded evacuation shelters is exponentially higher than during a lockdown in which the vast majority of people could stay at home. This issue would complicate evacuation procedures during the Californian wildfires in the second half of 2020.[81]

Others expressed concern about the implications of intersecting emergencies in future fire seasons. The pandemic had an adverse impact on firefighting capacity in the 2020 United States West Coast fires.[82] Incoming New South Wales Rural Fire Service Commissioner Rob Rogers, giving evidence in the Natural Disasters Royal Commission, pointed out that isolation requirements could dramatically reduce the numbers of available firefighters.[83] The pandemic also affected the availability of international firefighters to act as reinforcements;[84] during Black Summer, over 900 'specialist personnel' from New Zealand, Canada and the United States had contributed to firefighting operations.[85]

The inversion of climate narratives

Notwithstanding commonalities between the two phenomena, the onset of the pandemic distracted both governments and the Australian populace from the ominous implications of a warming climate. The pandemic created an alternate reality, in which the urgency of climate issues was downplayed and climate narratives were distorted or inverted. Joëlle Gergis has called this the sidelining of 'our collective trauma'.[86]

The message of intergenerational reproach, which distinguishes much youth climate activism and is encapsulated in the burgeoning school strike movement, lost ground to a new message of intergenerational care, and even sacrifice, on the part of members of Generation Z. Young people, including those who had thronged the streets of cities around the world during rolling school climate strikes in 2019, were expected to limit their activities in order to protect vulnerable elders. The complex nature of intergenerational responsibilities was underscored when triage practices in over-stretched medical facilities in Italy and Spain, during the first wave of the pandemic, raised concerns of age discrimination in relation to elderly patients.[87] Yet, throughout 2020, governments worldwide prioritised the pandemic emergency and economic recovery over the climate emergency, and thereby jeopardised the future wellbeing of today's youth: also a form of age discrimination.

Pandemic activism in public spaces became, ironically, the preserve of self-styled libertarians sponsored by right-wing groups, at least until the Black Lives Matter movement was galvanised into action in May. Climate activists complied with new social codes and, for the most part, confined their activities to the digital realm. Public expressions of protest acquired a new, potentially deadly significance. A rebuffing of the prime ministerial handshake, a powerful expression of individual defiance during the megafires, could be reinterpreted merely two months later as scrupulous adherence to new codes of social distancing.

The onset of the pandemic detracted from the palpable sense of urgency experienced during the megafires, and the new realisation of Australia's extreme climate vulnerability. Notwithstanding Morrison's bland assurance on New Year's Day 2020 that 'there's no better place to raise kids anywhere on the planet',[88] the megafires made it clear that Australia was in the frontline of climate change. During Black Summer, other nations viewed Australia's predicament from afar with pity and horror, as climate victim and climate scapegoat. Eminent climate scientist Michael Mann, on holiday in Australia during Black Summer before commencing a sabbatical, predicted that large areas of Australia would become uninhabitable.[89]

Yet, as Australia's response to the pandemic proved to be initially effective, a dangerous and unwarranted sense of complacency was revived, and internal narratives of Australia as lucky country and exemplary global citizen were reinstated. By April 2020, given Australia's relatively modest number of COVID-19 cases and low death tally, the Australian Chief Medical Officer could proclaim that 'there is no place in the world I would rather be than Australia at the moment'.[90] By May, the federal Health Minister was describing Australia as 'an island sanctuary'.[91]

A second wave, heralded by a sharp spike in cases and subsequent lockdown in Victoria, did not displace this new narrative; it seemed that other States could maintain a self-congratulatory tone while Melbourne featured in a 'cautionary tale that the rest of the country is scaring themselves with'.[92] Although some leaders cautioned against a sense of complacency at this point,[93] others encouraged it, with the Tasmanian Premier describing his State as 'one of the safest places in the world right now'.[94] In late October, when the Victorian lockdown ended amidst widespread relief, two health researchers commented that: 'No other place in the world has tamed a second wave this large. Few have even come close'.[95]

Another problematic narrative was also reinstated at this time: that of human mastery over natural phenomena. During Black Summer, there was a prevailing sense of powerlessness. The fires raged on, unstoppably, despite the herculean efforts of exhausted, largely voluntary firefighters; they were overcome only by heavy rain in February 2020. Humans may have become a geological force,[96] in large part through our excessive use of fossil fuels, but what we had seemingly unleashed could not be controlled or reined in. The megafires shattered the illusion of human mastery, the hubris underpinning the concept of the Anthropocene. In conjunction with other overwhelming disasters, they formed part of a 'language so powerful and expressive that human pretensions to mastery and control are shattered'.[97]

As Robyn Eckersley has pointed out, the dominant place of humans in the Anthropocene does not mean that other 'Earth-shaping forces' have been negated; these 'continue to amaze and confound us'.[98] Shortly after the megafires had been doused, Australians were forced to confront such a force: the COVID-19 virus. The virus served as a potent reminder, globally, that humans are not 'the only actors in the geological story'.[99] Yet, for Australia, geographical advantages, relatively prompt governmental intervention, widespread behavioural compliance and some degree of luck proved effective. The megafires highlighted our limitations, our vulnerability, our sense that, as one journalist put it, 'nature is closing in';[100] our success in vanquishing the virus suggested otherwise.

Emergency responses

The two phenomena triggered quite different political responses. Emergency measures adopted by State governments as a consequence of the megafires were short-lived and not particularly onerous for the Australian population. By way of contrast, the emergency measures rapidly introduced in response to the pandemic involved sweeping curtailment of certain well-entrenched rights – in particular, freedom of movement and freedom of assembly. Parliaments were suspended at both State and federal level. The executive arm of government was reinvigorated, with a newly created National Cabinet shaping Australia's overall response to the pandemic emergency. A National COVID-19 Coordination Commission, led by a former mining industry executive and with a 'handpicked membership . . . skewed towards people with links to fossil fuels',[101] played a key advisory role. The High Court stopped sitting in person; other courts conducted virtual hearings. Workplaces shut down or sent their employees home to work online. Unprecedented border closures impeded interstate travel and locked Australia away from the outside world.

Similar emergency measures, on a global scale, would contribute to a drop in greenhouse gas emissions. The International Energy Agency noted an initial, significant decline in global energy demand.[102] Authors of a study that spanned the first half of 2020 found that there was an 8.8% reduction in emissions relative to 2019 – the largest, absolute decrease in emissions ever recorded. Once lockdown measures were lifted, however, emissions increased.[103] In November, the Secretary-General of the World Meteorological Organisation called the initial decrease 'a tiny blip on the long-term graph'.[104]

In Australia, federal government endorsement of a 'gas-fired recovery',[105] with the strong encouragement of the National COVID-19 Coordination Commission,[106] boded ill for future climate mitigation measures. By July, researchers were describing Australia as an 'emissions superpower', the world's largest exporter of coal and gas.[107] In September, the federal government announced its support for a gas-fired power station in the Hunter Valley, five new gas fields and additional pipelines. In the same month, the New South Wales government provided a 'phased approval' for a highly controversial, coal seam gas project at Narrabri, subsequently also approved by the federal government, and the Queensland government approved a new coalmine in the Galilee Basin.

The perfect storm

The confluence of the megafires and the pandemic created a 'perfect storm': both extraordinary phenomena transforming Australian society, the Australian environment and the Australian psyche but also, potentially, the latter cancelling out or overshadowing the former. The grim repurposing of a Glasgow conference venue as a pandemic field hospital was an early indicator that the pandemic had, at least temporarily, superseded the climate crisis as a global emergency; the venue would have hosted a key climate summit, COP26, in November. Instead, participating countries and the United Nations decided to postpone the talks until 2021, with the United Kingdom energy minister explaining that the world's current focus was on 'saving lives and fighting Covid-19'.[108] Australian politician Zali Steggall announced in March that she would defer the introduction of her private Climate Change Bill, on the basis that the health crisis should take precedence;[109] the Bill,[110] which sets a net zero emissions target of 2050, was not introduced into the House of Representatives until early November.

The long-term consequences of the derailment and inversion of certain climate narratives during the pandemic were difficult to predict. In charting the impact of the megafires on the evolution of climate narratives in Australia, I have taken into consideration the points of intersection of these two catastrophic events, and their competing claims upon public audiences, public resources and the public imagination.

In Chapter 2, I address the extent to which the megafires contributed to a new apprehension of the climate emergency, and the ways in which the pandemic emergency influenced this process. My focus here is on the evolution of different narratives of emergency, including Indigenous narratives of emergency, throughout the year, and their broader implications.

Even before Black Summer ended, there was some preliminary discussion about grounds for lawsuits against those implicated in the catastrophe. In Chapter 3, drawing upon international and domestic precedents, I explore legal avenues open to claimants, climate lawsuits that commenced during 2020, and the broader significance of questions of culpability.

The fires began at the tail end of an extraordinary year in which climate activism became widely recognised as a powerful, global phenomenon. The fires further galvanised climate activists, both during Black Summer and immediately afterwards. The swift onset of the pandemic would, however, disrupt many planned events. In Chapter 4, I consider the ways in which the fires and the pandemic, and the problematic intersection of emergencies, shaped narratives of climate activism.

Finally, the uncanny parallels between climate and apocalyptic fiction and climate reality became apparent to many during the crisis. In the final chapter, I explore the interplay of fictitious narratives with the megafires, and the ways in which such narratives frame our experience of such climate disasters and anticipate and reflect our responses.

Anthropocene framings and scalar limitations

I deploy herein a unique, interdisciplinary methodology that is a tapestried approach, woven from multiple perspectives and associated theories, methods and empirical observations. I have been influenced by recent developments in critical legal, literary and political studies, and my work is informed by eco-philosophical insights concerning human-nature relations. I reject a post-truth perspective that dismisses or downplays scientific knowledge but, instead, draw upon current findings in climate science; these findings frame my understanding of the material realities of the climate emergency, and its current and projected consequences for planetary health and wellbeing.

In this project, I draw extensively upon the work of Timothy Clark, Timothy Morton and Amitav Ghosh on Anthropocene framings and scalar limitations.[111] These theorists highlight the scalar deficiencies of existing literary modes and, indeed, modes of thinking and behaving, in contending with the enormity of what Morton calls hyperobjects: phenomena, such as climate change, 'that are massively distributed in time and space relative to humans'.[112] The multiple scales at work generate what historian Dipesh Charkrabarty calls 'rifts' in our thinking: 'we have to keep crossing or straddling them as we think or speak of climate change'.[113]

Chakrabarty's 2009 essay[114] on the geological significance of humanity as a species attracted considerable ire from some commentators in the humanities;[115] their concerns coalesced around the inequalities and injustices that are arguably glossed over in this seemingly essentialist argument. In fact, Chakrabarty later emphasised the key importance of zooming in, to ensure that issues of intra-species justice, the 'human inequality and suffering caused by modern institutions', are not disregarded, as well as zooming out, to acknowledge the global and planetary impacts of humanity on the Earth system.[116] I make use of his metaphor in my analysis.

The dominant climate narratives of 2020, narratives of emergency, of lawfulness and culpability, of activism, of fictitious apocalypse, illustrate some of the challenges in achieving such deliberately doubled vision. Temporal and spatial considerations shape our conception of emergency and hinder our capacity to rally in response to planetary forces. Established narratives of lawfulness and culpability also reflect our predilection for zooming in rather than zooming out. Issues of rights, fairness and justice shaped the protest narratives of 2020, and arguably detracted from an earlier, overriding emphasis on the planetary climate emergency; a splintering and diluting effect became evident. Finally, in narratives of fiction, it is difficult to portray the 'leviathon of humanity';[117] writers of realist fiction zoom in. Even in the increasingly popular genre of apocalyptic fiction, individual stories predominate. And yet, despite the focus upon the fate of individuals, a number of common themes recur in such texts. By reflecting back to us our concerns and preoccupations about a looming climate apocalypse, fictitious narratives can enable the reader to broaden his or her perspective beyond the parochial.

The megafires, in conjunction with the pandemic, offered Australians an unprecedented opportunity to reflect upon and address two emergencies that intersected at a planetary scale. The popular, political, legal, activist and literary narratives that framed and constituted our response are considered in the following chapters.

Notes

1 Katharine Murphy, 'Dear Michael McCormack: The Only Raving Lunatics Are Those Not Worrying about Climate Change', *The Guardian* (online, 11 November 2019) <www.theguardian.com/australia-news/2019/nov/11/dear-michael-mccormack-the-only-raving-lunatics-are-those-not-worrying-about-climate-change>.

2 Emma Elsworthy, 'Liberal MPs Matt Kean and Sussan Ley Link Bushfires to Climate Change', *ABC News* (online, 11 December 2019) <www.abc.net.au/news/2019-12-11/matt-kean-blames-bushfires-on-climate-change/11787498>; David Crowe, 'Liberals Speak Out to Back Science

Minister on Climate Change Action', *The Sydney Morning Herald* (online, 15 January 2020) <www.smh.com.au/politics/federal/liberals-speak-out-to-back-science-minister-on-climate-change-action-20200115-p53rs1.html>.

3 Amy Remeikis, 'Morrison Responds to Fears over Bushfires But Rejects Censure of Climate Policy', *The Guardian* (online, 12 December 2019) <www.theguardian.com/australia-news/2019/dec/12/morrison-responds-to-fears-over-bushfires-but-rejects-censure-of-climate-policy>.

4 Peter Hannam, '"We're Bloody Lucky We Didn't Bury Thousands of People": Constance's New Climate Pledge', *The Sydney Morning Herald* (online, 12 October 2020) <www.smh.com.au/environment/climate-change/we-re-bloody-lucky-we-didn-t-bury-thousands-of-people-constance-s-new-climate-pledge-20201009-p563lk.html>.

5 Evidence to Royal Commission into National Natural Disaster Arrangements, Canberra, 25 May 2020, 22 (Dr Karl Braganza).

6 Ibid 11.

7 *Royal Commission into National Natural Disaster Arrangements* (Final Report, 28 October 2020) 55.

8 Ibid.

9 *Final Report of the NSW Bushfire Inquiry* (31 July 2020) iv.

10 Geert Jan Van Oldenborgh et al, 'Attribution of the Australian Bushfire Risk to Anthropogenic Climate Change' (2020) *Natural Hazards and Earth System Sciences* <https://doi.org/10.5194/nhess-2020-69>.

11 Brendan Mackey et al, *Bushfire Science Report No 1: Does Climate Change Affect Bushfire Risks in the Native Forests of Eastern Australia?* (Report, Bushfire Recovery Project, 2020) 7 <www.bushfirefacts.org/report-1.html>.

12 Nerilie J Abram et al, 'Connections of Climate Change and Variability to Large and Extreme Forest Fires in Southeast Australia' (2021) 2 *Communications Earth and Environment* 8:1–17, 12 <https://doi.org/10.1038/s43247-020-00065-8>.

13 Tracy Bowden, 'Quiet Australians Decide It Is Time to Speak Up on Climate Change Action', *ABC News* (online, 29 January 2020) <www.abc.net.au/news/2020-01-29/new-activists-quiet-australians-government-action-climate-change/11903728>.

14 Rob Harris, 'Can Scott Morrison Seize This Watershed Moment for Climate Policy?', *Brisbane Times* (online, 17 January 2020) <www.brisbanetimes.com.au/politics/federal/can-scott-morrison-seize-this-watershed-moment-for-climate-policy-20200117-p53se6.html>.

15 The Australia Institute, *Climate of the Nation 2020: Tracking Australia's Attitudes towards Climate Change and Energy* (Report, October 2020) 10.

16 Ibid 4.

17 Ibid 7.

18 Steven Sherwood et al, *An Open Letter on Australian Bushfires and Climate: Urgent Need for Deep Cuts in Carbon Emissions* <https://laureatebushfiresclimate.wordpress.com>.

19 Lesley Hughes et al, *Summer of Crisis* (Report, Climate Council, 2020) 7.

20 Oldenborgh et al (n 10).

21 Hughes et al (n 19) 11.

22 Ibid 12.

23 Ibid 7.

24 Ibid.

25 Keven Nguyen, Philippa McDonald and Maryanne Taouk, 'Anatomy of a "Mega-Blaze"', *ABC News* (online, 27 July 2020) <www.abc.net.au/news/2020-07-27/gospers-mountain-mega-blaze-investigation/12472044>.

26 Timothy Clark, *Ecocriticism on the Edge: The Anthropocene as a Threshold Concept* (Bloomsbury Publishing, 2015) 13.

27 Ibid 30.

28 Ibid.

29 Bevan Shields and Matthew Knott, '"Stop Us in Our Tracks": Biden's New Climate Chief John Kerry Invokes Australian Bushfires', *The Sydney Morning Herald* (online, 28 January 2021) <www.smh.com.au/world/europe/stop-us-in-our-tracks-biden-s-new-climate-chief-john-kerry-invokes-australian-bushfires-20210128-p56xce.html>.

30 'Australia Fires: Smoke to Make "Full Circuit" around Globe, NASA Says', *BBC News* (online, 14 January 2020) <www.bbc.com/news/world-australia-51101049>.

31 Sergey Khaykin et al, 'The 2019/20 Australian Wildfires Generated a Persistent Smoke-Charged Vortex Rising up to 35 Km Altitude' (2020) *Communications Earth and Environment* 22:1–12, 1 <https://doi.org/10.1038/s43247-020-00022-5>.

32 Quoted in Lisa Cox, 'Smoke Cloud from Australian Summer's Bushfires Three-Times Larger Than Anything Previously Recorded', *The Guardian* (online, 3 November 2020) <www.theguardian.com/australia-news/2020/nov/03/smoke-cloud-from-australian-summers-bushfires-three-times-larger-than-anything-previously-recorded>.

33 Maddie Stone, 'Australia's Black Summer Bushfires Acted Like a Volcanic Eruption, Slightly Cooling the Globe', *The Age* (online, 13 December 2020) <www.theage.com.au/environment/climate-change/australia-s-severe-2019-20-bushfires-acted-like-a-volcanic-eruption-slightly-cooling-the-globe-20201213-p56mzj.html>.

34 John Pickrell, 'Thousands of Ancient Aboriginal Sites Probably Damaged in Australian Fires' (23 January 2020) *Nature* <www.nature.com/articles/d41586-020-00164-8>.

35 Quoted in Calla Wahlquist, '"Brutal Business": Bushfire Devastation Causes "Collective Grief" among Wildlife Carers', *The Guardian* (online, 17 January 2020) <www.theguardian.com/australia-news/2020/jan/17/brutal-business-bushfire-devastation-causes-collective-grief-among-wildlife-carers>.

36 Douglas Kahn, 'What Is an Ecopath?' (3 March 2020) *Sydney Review of Books* <https://sydneyreviewofbooks.com/essay/what-is-an-ecopath>.

37 Brendan A Wintle, Sarah Legge and John CZ Woinarski, 'After the Megafires: What Next for Australian Wildlife?' (2020) 35 *Trends in Ecology and Evolution* 753, 753.

38 Ibid 754.

39 Ibid 755.

40 Lily Van Eeden et al, *Impacts of the Unprecedented 2019–2020 Bushfires on Australian Animals* (Report, World Wide Fund for Nature Australia, November 2020) 7.

41 Ibid 21.

42 Quoted in Graham Readfearn and Adam Morton, ‘Almost 3 Billion Animals Affected by Australian Bushfires, Report Shows’, *The Guardian* (online, 28 July 2020) <www.theguardian.com/environment/2020/jul/28/almost-3-billion-animals-affected-by-australian-megafires-report-shows-aoe>.

43 Michael Curtin et al, ‘The Impact of Bushfire on the Wellbeing of Children Living in Rural and Remote Australia’ (2020) 213(S11) *The Medical Journal of Australia* 14.

44 Sophie C Lewis, ‘This Is What Climate Change Looks Like’, *Sophie C Lewis Climate Scientist* (Blog Post, 20 January 2020) <https://sophieclewis.com/2020/01/20/this-is-what-climate-change-looks-like>.

45 Nicholas Biddle et al, ‘Exposure and the Impact on Attitudes of the 2019–20 Australian Bushfires’ (Research Paper, Australian National University Centre for Social Research and Methods, 2020) 4 <https://csrm.cass.anu.edu.au/sites/default/files/docs/2020/5/Exposure_and_impact_on_attitudes_of_the_2019-20_Australian_Bushfires_publication.pdf>.

46 Nicholas Borchers Arriagada et al, ‘Unprecedented Smoke-Related Health Burden Associated with the 2019–20 Bushfires in Eastern Australia’ (2020) 213(6) *The Medical Journal of Australia* 282.

47 Peter Hannam, ‘Sydney Water Quality Issues Keep Desal Plant Running’, *The Sydney Morning Herald* (online, 14 August 2020) <www.smh.com.au/environment/conservation/sydney-water-quality-issues-keep-desal-plant-running-20200813-p55lfw.html>.

48 Peter Hannam, ‘Australia’s Emissions to Push Global Emissions to New High: Met Office’, *The Sydney Morning Herald* (online, 24 January 2020) <www.smh.com.au/environment/climate-change/australia-s-bushfires-to-push-global-emissions-to-new-high-met-office-20200124-p53ub2.html>.

49 Australian Trade and Investment Commission, *Global Sentiment Monitor: Tracking the World’s Perception of Australia after the Bushfires* (Report, 2020) 3.

50 Ibid 7.

51 Brigid Delaney, ‘Fire Raining on Beaches, Red Skies and a Billion Animals Killed: The New Australian Summer’, *The Guardian* (online, 24 January 2020) <www.theguardian.com/commentisfree/2020/jan/23/fire-raining-on-beaches-red-skies-and-a-billion-animals-killed-the-new-australian-summer>.

52 Deborah Snow, Peter Hannam and Natassia Chrysanthos, ‘“Australia’s First Climate Refugees”’, *The Sydney Morning Herald* (online, 4 January 2020) <www.smh.com.au/national/australia-s-first-climate-change-refugees-20200103-p53okp.html>.

53 Quoted in Nick Miller, ‘Award-Winning Oz Filmmaker Attacks “Dinosaur Ally” Morrison at Davos’, *The Sydney Morning Herald* (online, 21 January 2020) <www.smh.com.au/culture/movies/award-winning-oz-filmmaker-attacks-dinosaur-ally-morrison-at-davos-20200121-p53te6.html>.

54 Joëlle Gergis, ‘The Great Unravelling’ in Sophie Cunningham (ed), *Fire, Flood and Plague: Australian Writers Respond to 2020* (Vintage Books, 2020) 44, 47.

55 Oliver Milman, ‘Pacific Islands Make Last-Ditch Plea to World before Paris Climate Change Talks’, *The Guardian* (online, 2 November 2015) <www.theguardian.com/environment/2015/nov/02/pacific-islands-make-last-ditch-plea-to-world-before-paris-climate-change-talks>.

56 Robert Aisi, 'Facing Extinction: Climate Change and the Threat to Pacific Island Countries' (2007) 90 *Reform* 65, 67.
57 David Wallace-Wells, 'U.N. Climate Talks Collapsed in Madrid: What's the Way Forward?' (16 December 2019) *New York* <http://nymag.com/intelligencer/2019/12/cop25-ended-in-failure-whats-the-way-forward.html>.
58 Oliver Milman, 'California Wildfires Spawn First "Gigafire" in Modern History', *The Guardian* (online, 7 October 2020) <www.theguardian.com/us-news/2020/oct/06/california-wildfires-gigafire-first>. A gigafire spans more than one million acres.
59 These included the Vanuatan, Fijian and Papua New Guinean governments.
60 Judith Brett, 'The Coal Curse: Resources, Climate and Australia's Future' (June 2020, Issue 78) *Quarterly Essay* 5.
61 Ibid 4–5.
62 *Paris Agreement*, opened for signature 22 April 2016, 2016 ATS 24 (entered into force 4 November 2016).
63 Quoted in Nick O'Malley, 'World Awaits Action by "Suicidal" Australia, Says Former Climate Chief', *The Age* (online, 1 December 2020) <www.theage.com.au/environment/climate-change/world-awaits-action-by-suicidal-australia-says-former-climate-chief-20201201-p56joj.html>.
64 Richard Flanagan, 'Australia Is Committing Climate Suicide', *The New York Times* (online, 3 January 2020) <www.nytimes.com/2020/01/03/opinion/australia-fires-climate-change.html>.
65 See, eg, Lesley Head, 'Transformative Change Requires Resisting a New Normal' (2020) 10 *Nature Climate Change* 173, 174.
66 Thomas Keneally, 'Thomas Keneally: "These Fires Have Changed Us"', *The Guardian* (online, 1 February 2020) <www.theguardian.com/australia-news/2020/feb/01/thomas-keneally-these-fires-have-changed-us>.
67 Kim Stanley Robinson, *The Ministry for the Future* (Orbit, 2020) 231–3.
68 Ibid 125.
69 Livia Albeck-Ripka, '"A Nightmare": Losing a Home to Australia's Fires, Then Locked Down by a Virus', *The New York Times* (online, 10 May 2020) <www.nytimes.com/2020/05/10/world/australia/coronavirus-bushfires.html>.
70 Sophie Cunningham, 'If You Choose to Stay, We May Not Be Able to Save You' (Winter 2020) *Meanjin* <https://meanjin.com.au/essays/if-you-choose-to-stay-we-may-not-be-able-to-save-you>.
71 Christos Tsiolkas, 'Call and Response' in Cunningham (n 54) 101, 104.
72 Andreas Malm, *Corona, Climate and Chronic Emergency: War Communism in the Twenty-First Century* (Verso, 2020) 81.
73 Ibid 24.
74 Aletheia Casey, 'Lost Land' (May 2020) *Emergence Magazine* <https://emergencemagazine.org/story/lost-land>.
75 Jennifer Mills, 'Trouble Breathing' in Cunningham (n 54) 145, 146.
76 Kate Galloway, 'There's No Place Like Home' (2020) 30(9) *Eureka Street* <www.eurekastreet.com.au/article/there-s-no-place-like-home>.
77 Jilly Boyce Kay, '"Stay the Fuck at Home!": Feminism, Family and the Private Home in a Time of Coronavirus' (2020) 20(6) *Feminist Media Studies* 883, 887.
78 This is discussed further in chapter five.
79 Jennifer Mills, 'The Rhythms of These Numberless Days' (3 April 2020) *Meanjin* <https://meanjin.com.au/blog/the-rhythms-of-these-numberless-days>.

80 Carly A Phillips et al, 'Compound Climate Risks in the COVID-19 Pandemic' (2020) 10 *Nature Climate Change* 586.

81 Maanvi Singh, 'California Wildfires: Rapidly Growing Blazes Force Thousands to Flee', *The Guardian* (online, 21 August 2020) <www.theguardian.com/us-news/2020/aug/20/california-wildfires-latest-lightning-fire-bay-area>.

82 Gabrielle Canon, 'Firefighters Pushed to the Limits as Unprecedented Infernos Rage across US West Coast', *The Guardian* (online, 15 September 2020) <www.theguardian.com/world/2020/sep/15/firefighters-pushed-to-the-limits-as-unprecedented-infernos-rage-across-us-west-coast>.

83 Evidence to Royal Commission into National Natural Disaster Arrangements, Canberra, 15 July 2020, 2004 (Rob Rogers).

84 Ibid 1965.

85 Ibid 1964.

86 Gergis (n 54) 48.

87 See Sabine Michalowski, 'The Use of Age as a Triage Criterion' in Carla Ferstman and Andew Fagan (eds), *Covid-19, Law and Human Rights: Essex Dialogues* (University of Essex, 1 July 2020) 93, 93–4.

88 Quoted in Amy Remeikis, '"No Better Place to Raise Kids": Scott Morrison's New Year Message to a Burning Australia' (1 January 2020) *The Guardian* <www.theguardian.com/australia-news/2020/jan/01/no-better-place-to-raise-kids-scott-morrison-new-year-message-burning-australia>.

89 Matthew Burgess, 'Australia's Bushfires May Create the Nation's First Climate Refugees' (24 January 2020) *Time* <https://time.com/5770902/australia-wildfires-climate-refugees>.

90 Quoted in Colin Brinsden, 'Australia in "Good Place", Says CMO', *The Canberra Times* (online, 12 April 2020) <www.canberratimes.com.au/story/6719793/australia-in-good-place-says-cmo>.

91 Quoted in Sherryn Groch, 'Second Wave or Just Ripples: What Next for the Pandemic?', *The Sydney Morning Herald* (online, 30 May 2020) <www.smh.com.au/national/second-wave-ripples-or-flare-ups-what-next-for-the-pandemic-20200526-p54wph.html>.

92 Sophie Black, 'Victoria's Coronavirus Crisis: Fear Hangs over Melbourne and Nothing Is Like the First Wave', *The Guardian* (online, 1 August 2020) <www.theguardian.com/australia-news/commentisfree/2020/aug/01/victorias-coronavirus-crisis-fear-hangs-over-melbourne-and-nothing-is-like-the-first-wave>.

93 NSW Government, 'One Million COVID-19 Tests But No Room for Complacency' (Media Release, 10 July 2020) <www.nsw.gov.au/media-releases/one-million-covid-19-tests-but-no-room-for-complacency>.

94 Quoted in Cas Garvey, 'Premier Peter Gutwein Reveals Tassie's Border Opening Plans', *The Mercury* (online, 27 July 2020) <www.themercury.com.au/news/tasmania/premier-peter-gutwein-reveals-tassies-border-opening-plans/news-story/f4f92157de2490cca28649036ef4cb94>.

95 Stephen Duckett and Tom Crowley, 'Finally at Zero New Cases, Victoria Is on Top of the World after Unprecedented Lockdown Effort', *The Conversation* (online, 26 October 2020) <https://theconversation.com/finally-at-zero-new-cases-victoria-is-on-top-of-the-world-after-unprecedented-lockdown-effort-148808>.

96 Dipesh Chakrabarty, 'The Climate of History: Four Theses' (2009) 35(2) *Critical Inquiry* 197, 206.

97 Deborah Bird Rose, 'Anthropocene Noir' (2013–14) 41/42 *Arena* 206, 209.
98 Robyn Eckersley, 'Geopolitan Democracy in the Anthropocene' (2017) 65(4) *Political Studies* 983, 989.
99 Ibid.
100 Damien Cave, 'The End of Australia as We Know It', *The New York Times* (online, 15 February 2020) <www.nytimes.com/2020/02/15/world/australia/fires-climate-change.html>.
101 Brett (n 60) 74.
102 International Energy Agency, *Global Energy Review 2020: The Impacts of the Covid-19 Crisis on Global Energy Demand and CO2 Emissions* (Report, April 2020) <www.iea.org/reports/global-energy-review-2020>.
103 Zhu Liu et al, 'Near-Real-Time Monitoring of Global CO_2 Emissions Reveals the Effect of the COVID-19 Pandemic' (2020) 11 *Nature Communications* 5172:1–12, 7 <https://doi.org/10.1038/s41467-020-18922-7>.
104 Quoted in Damian Carrington, 'Climate Crisis: CO2 Hits New Record Despite Covid-19 Lockdowns', *The Guardian* (online, 23 November 2020) <www.theguardian.com/environment/2020/nov/23/climate-crisis-co2-hits-new-record-despite-covid-19-lockdowns>.
105 Mike Foley, 'Gas to Fire Economic Recovery and Capitalise on Cheap Oil Prices', *The Sydney Morning Herald* (online, 21 April 2020) <www.smh.com.au/politics/federal/gas-to-fire-economic-recovery-and-capitalise-on-cheap-oil-prices-20200421-p54lw8.html>.
106 Nick Bonyhady and Mike Foley, 'COVID Taskforce Urges Government Support for New Gas Projects', *The Sydney Morning Herald* (online, 29 July 2020) <www.smh.com.au/politics/federal/covid-taskforce-urges-government-support-for-new-gas-projects-20200728-p55g8q.html>.
107 Jeremy Moss, *Australia: An Emissions Super-Power* (Report, Practical Justice Initiative, University of New South Wales, July 2020) 3 <https://climatejustice.co/wp-content/uploads/2020/07/Australia-_-an-emissions-super-power.pdf>.
108 Quoted in Jillian Ambrose and Fiona Harvey, 'COP26 Climate Talks in Glasgow Postponed Until 2021', *The Guardian* (online, 2 April 2020) <www.theguardian.com/environment/2020/apr/01/uk-likely-to-postpone-cop26-un-climate-talks-glasgow-coronavirus>.
109 Lachlan Moffet Gray, 'Zali Steggall to Delay Her Climate Change Bill, Saying MPs Must Focus on Coronavirus', *The Australian* (online, 17 March 2020) <www.theaustralian.com.au/nation/zali-steggall-to-delay-her-climate-change-bill-saying-mps-must-focus-on-coronavirus/news-story/8955de98687b580414c62e391645e99d>.
110 Climate Change (National Framework for Adaptation and Mitigation) Bill 2020 (Cth).
111 See Clark (n 26); Timothy Morton, *Hyperobjects: Philosophy and Ecology after the End of the World* (University of Minnesota Press, 2013); Amitav Ghosh, *The Great Derangement: Climate Change and the Unthinkable* (University of Chicago Press, 2016).
112 Morton (n 111) 1.
113 Dipesh Chakrabarty, 'Climate and Capital: On Conjoined Histories' (2014) 41(1) *Critical Inquiry* 1, 3.
114 Chakrabarty (n 96).

115 See, eg, Robert Emmett and Thomas Lekan (eds), *Whose Anthropocene? Revisiting Dipesh Chakrabarty's 'Four Theses'* (RCC Perspectives, Transformations in Environment and Society, 2016).
116 Dipesh Chakrabarty, 'The Human Significance of the Anthropocene' in Bruno Latour and Christophe Leclercq (eds), *Reset Modernity!* (MIT Press, 2016) 189, 198.
117 Clark (n 26) 73.

2 Narratives of emergency

Nicole Rogers

In 2019, the term 'climate emergency' entered the political lexicon. It dominated popular discourse to such a degree that it became the Oxford Dictionary's word of the year. Numerous governments at local, city and national levels made declarations of climate emergency. The Pope acknowledged a climate emergency in June.[1] In November, over 11,000 scientists from around the world 'clearly and unequivocally' endorsed a declaration 'that planet Earth is facing a climate emergency'.[2]

Emergency responses at governmental level were, however, conspicuously absent. Significantly, there was no attempt at curtailment of the rights enjoyed by individual and corporate beneficiaries of the post-World War II exponential growth in both international human rights law and transnational corporate domination. This period, in light of the steep rise in greenhouse gas emissions and dramatic change in the magnitude and rate of the human imprint on the Earth system, has been described by climate scientist Will Steffen and his colleagues as 'the Great Acceleration'.[3]

As already highlighted in the previous chapter, Black Summer heightened awareness of the imminence and magnitude of the climate emergency, both in Australia and elsewhere. In February 2020, in the immediate aftermath of the fires, a National Climate Emergency Summit was held in the Melbourne Town Hall; this culminated in a Safe Climate Declaration.[4] Signatories called for all levels of government to oversee an emergency transition to a safe climate and prioritise climate action over other policies, while simultaneously strengthening democracy and citizens' rights. Later in 2020, building upon the emergency declarations of the previous year, 64 leaders from five countries signed a statement in which they acknowledged the existence of a planetary emergency, encompassing the climate crisis and biodiversity loss, and emphasised the need for transformative change.[5] Speaking at a virtual Climate Ambition Summit in December, the Secretary-General of the United Nations urged every country to enact 'a state of climate emergency'.[6]

DOI: 10.4324/b22677-2

The Australian government continued, for the most part, to disregard such developments. A Climate Emergency Declaration Bill, introduced into the House of Representatives by the Australian Greens leader in March 2019, failed to pass through Parliament. The government's response to the megafires was reactive, focused upon adaptation rather than mitigation. Throughout 2020, the Prime Minister stubbornly refused to change Australia's climate policies or set net zero emissions targets,[7] in marked contrast to other wealthy nations including the United Kingdom, China, South Korea and Japan. The government's reactive response was at odds with the conclusion of its own Natural Disasters Royal Commission that '[a] resilient nation will seek to mitigate the risk of disasters through a wide range of measures'.[8]

Yet is it possible for governments to acknowledge and respond effectively to the climate emergency, or indeed any emergency, without sacrificing the democratic freedoms and rights of its citizens? This question would be raised in numerous contexts and fora throughout 2020. It is a version of what Jocelyn Stacey, in her discussion of the environmental emergency, has called Schmitt's emergency challenge: the challenge of demonstrating whether and, if so, how emergencies can be governed by law.[9] Carl Schmitt, a German theorist and Nazi supporter, believed that emergencies are distinguished by the unfettered and exceptional exercise of executive power and that, furthermore, the exercise of such power is not subject to legal constraints. He argued that the exception lies outside the legal order; the rule of law is not applicable within the framework of the exception.[10]

In this chapter, I interrogate the narratives of emergency foregrounded by the extraordinary events of 2020. In Australia, such narratives surfaced as part of political discourse, accompanying the governmental response to the megafires, the pandemic and the economic ramifications of both. I discuss the significance of the palpable but relatively short-term emergency of the megafires in shaping understandings of the chronic climate emergency, and consider whether these lessons were reinforced, superseded or even undermined by the pandemic emergency that followed. I reflect upon the implications of pandemic restrictions for the introduction of restrictions and curtailments that are, arguably, a necessary part of responding to the climate emergency and, in addition, a likely consequence or outcome of that emergency.

In the final part of the chapter, I turn to Indigenous narratives of emergency, and the impacts of the megafires, and climate emergency generally, on Aboriginal people.

Emergency and the rule of law

Schmitt described the state of exception, or emergency, as characterised by 'the suspension of the entire existing order'; he continued: '[i]n such a situation it is clear that the state remains, whereas law recedes'.[11] During the so-called War on Terror, which brought a loss of liberties, an unprecedented level of executive control and a 'recasting of the balance between the executive and judicial arms of government'[12] for countries in the Global North, Schmitt's thesis on the state of exception enjoyed a 'timely or untimely renaissance'.[13] Most notably, eminent theorist Giorgio Agamben was accused of an uncritical engagement with Schmitt's theory of exception.[14] Agamben endorsed Schmitt's position, asserting that the state of exception brought with it 'a suspension of the juridical order'.[15]

Tom Cohen has suggested that the war on terror deflected attention away from the far more ominous, existential threat of climate change: a '*threat without enemy*'.[16] In the first decade of the twenty-first century, theorists and commentators pondered at length upon the implications of the putative state of exception engendered by the war on terror; they omitted, for the most part, to speculate on the dimensions of a future state of exception ushered in by the climate emergency. Writing in 2010, however, Bruce Lindsay embarked upon an analysis of ways in which emergency responses to the climate crisis could be incorporated within the Australian legal system. He observed that the concept of climate emergency represented 'a new *form* of declared emergency'; existing emergency models did not suffice.[17]

Lindsay identified one distinguishing feature of the climate emergency, in contrast to other emergencies: its 'highly (although not exclusively) prospective character'. Thus, he wrote, it necessitates 'pre-emptive or anticipatory, rather than reactive or defensive, measures'.[18] By 2020, this statement required revision; although anticipatory measures were still imperative, it was evident that the climate emergency was happening in real time. The megafires were a potent, present manifestation of climate emergency and harbinger of future, increasingly more extreme, climate-related emergencies. Other climate-related disasters punctuated the year, including catastrophic fires elsewhere in the world: the Amazon, Siberia and the West Coast of the United States.

A perceived disjunction between such short-lived, extreme emergencies and the unending, accelerating, planetary emergency of climate change explains, in part, the disparity between conventional legal responses to emergencies such as natural disasters, and the jarring absence of response to the climate emergency. Federal, State and Territory governments, reluctant to place Australia on an emergency footing in order to address the planetary climate crisis, displayed no such hesitation when confronted with the relatively short-term emergencies of Black Summer and the pandemic. As became clear throughout 2020, there is statutory provision at State and Territory levels and, to a more limited extent, at Commonwealth level for the imposition of states of emergency, and the corresponding conferral of special powers upon the executive arms of government.[19] As also became clear, Australian governments are quite prepared to invoke these provisions.

From a Schmittian perspective, the existence of such legislation poses a conundrum. If emergency necessitates a setting aside of the rule of law, how can the legal system accommodate and acknowledge the existence of emergencies, and authorise the exercise of enhanced, arbitrary, special powers by the executive arm of government during such periods? This could, perhaps, be explained by what Agamben depicts as a relationship of mutual dependency, in which the judicial order 'must seek in every way to assure itself a relation' with this 'space devoid of law'.[20] Such provisions could also be viewed as an attempt by the legal order to counter the threat of the extra-legal through what Roberto Esposito has called the 'immunitary mechanism': the law 'reproduc[ing] in a controlled form exactly what it is meant to protect us from'.[21]

It has been suggested that the effectiveness of any definitional or procedural safeguards in civil emergency and special powers statutes rests upon their enforceability, and the overall justiceability of emergency powers.[22] The enforceability of such statutory measures in a crisis becomes a moot point if Schmitt's thesis is correct, and emergency powers cannot be constrained by law.[23] Statutory provisions in relation to emergency can operate as problematic legal grey holes, to adopt the terminology of David Dyzenhaus: far more dangerous, in his view, than legal black holes.[24] According to Dyzenhaus, their function is to 'place a thin veneer of legality on the political';[25] to create the 'pretence of legality'.[26] He suggests that judges should refrain from adjudicating on the exercise of certain executive powers, if the only outcome would be 'an empty proceduralism'.[27]

In the following sections, I elaborate upon the use of statutory emergency provisions by State, Territory and federal governments during Black Summer, and subsequently throughout 2020, and the extent to which these were subject to judicial oversight.

States of emergency and the megafires

Throughout the terrible spring and summer of 2019 and 2020, the governments of the worst affected States and the Australian Capital Territory made various declarations of emergency.[28] The New South Wales government made three such declarations, each lasting one week, under the *State of Emergency and Rescue Management Act 1989* (NSW). The Rural Fires Service Commissioner was thereby empowered to, inter alia, forcibly evacuate people, take possession of property and close roads.[29] There had been only four prior declarations of emergency in the State since 2006.

In November 2019, Queensland declared a State of Fire Emergency under the *Fire and Emergency Services Act 1990* (Qu);[30] consequently, the Commissioner could take 'any reasonable measure to abate the fire emergency'.[31] It was revoked after a fortnight, when conditions eased in the State. Queensland also has a *Disaster Management Act 2003* (Qld), which activates certain disaster powers once a 'disaster situation' is declared by certain designated individuals, including the responsible Minister and the Premier. This particular declaration was not made during Black Summer, although an extended disaster situation was imposed in 2020 in response to the pandemic.

In the case of Victoria, there was, for the first time, a declaration of a state of disaster for some bushfire-affected regions;[32] this remained in force for seven days in early January. The declaration was consistent with one of the recommendations of the 2009 Victorian Bushfires Royal Commission[33] and bestowed extensive powers upon the relevant Minister. The Minister could take possession and make use of any person's property; control and restrict entry into, movement within and departure from the disaster area; and compel evacuation from the area.[34] In addition, he or she had the power to suspend the operation of any Act or regulation that in his/her view would inhibit the response to or recovery from the disaster.[35] According to the 2009 Royal Commission, the symbolic importance of such a declaration during a catastrophic bushfire, and the potential reassurance provided to the public by the assumption of control by the State's political leaders, were as significant as the coercive powers conferred.[36]

Finally, at the end of January 2020, the Australian Capital Territory upgraded an existing state of alert to a three-day state of emergency under its *Emergencies Act 2004* (ACT),[37] thereby triggering the exercise of a range of emergency powers by the emergency controller.[38]

In contrast to these declarations at State and Territory level, there was no declaration of a state of national emergency by the Commonwealth government. The Commonwealth's role in relation to natural or man-made civil emergencies has historically involved the provision of financial and logistical assistance to State governments, while the States bear primary responsibility for managing the emergency.[39] There is no specific provision in the Australian constitutional framework for declarations of emergency at the federal level.[40] Nevertheless, the Commonwealth has increasingly used certain legislative and executive emergency powers to deal with emergencies of national significance, drawing upon rationales such as national preservation.[41]

The constitutionality of a declaration of national emergency, as an exercise of the Commonwealth's executive or legislative powers, was one of the matters considered by the 2020 Natural Disasters Royal Commission. The Commission recommended that the Commonwealth enact legislation that conferred the power to declare a national emergency, including in 'limited' circumstances in which the States did not request assistance.[42] In late 2020, the federal government put forward a National Emergency Declaration Bill, which passed through both Houses of Parliament in December. This followed spirited discussion in the party room about the triggers for such a declaration; the potential overreach of executive power; and the possibility, unpalatable to the then government, that one of their successors might use the legislation to declare a climate emergency.[43] The legislation confers power upon the Governor-General, acting upon the advice of the Prime Minister, to make a national emergency declaration in certain scenarios, including when it is deemed appropriate in light of 'the nature of the emergency and the nature and severity of the nationally significant harm'.[44] A requirement for prior consultation with the States and Territories can be disregarded if the Prime Minister is 'satisfied that it is not practicable' to carry out the consultation process.[45]

The divergence in approach between the Commonwealth government and State and Territory governments during Black Summer highlighted what was perceived, at the time, as a crisis in national leadership. In the interim report of a 2020 Senate inquiry into the fires, the Committee observed that there was a 'lack of clarity' about 'what the Prime Minister knew and when, and what actions he took upon receiving advice about the unfolding bushfire disaster'.[46] He notoriously left the country in December for an overseas holiday, returning only in the face of a public outcry; this has been described as one of 'the most unfortunate political missteps in recent history'.[47] The subsequent deployment of 3000 army reservists in early January, the largest deployment for a natural disaster since Cyclone Tracy in 1974, was announced by the Commonwealth government without prior consultation with the States.[48] A promotional video, released immediately afterwards from the Prime Minister's office, attracted widespread condemnation for its hyperbolic portrayal of the government's response to the bushfires.[49] Footage of exhausted firefighters and survivors, rebuking Morrison for his apparent indifference, went viral.[50]

The Commonwealth government also drew criticism for its earlier downgrading of the role of Emergency Management Australia, the Commonwealth agency tasked with disaster management and coordination of requests from States and Territories for emergency assistance. The agency was subsumed within the Department of Home Affairs in 2018. In his evidence to the Royal Commission, Greg Mullins, outspoken former Commissioner of Fire and Rescue NSW, expressed concern that it thereafter lacked direct access to the Prime Minister or Cabinet; in his view, this impeded rapid decision-making at the national level in response to the fires.[51]

In its final Report, released in October, the Natural Disasters Royal Commission acknowledged the importance of effective national coordination in the management of natural disasters, and proposed 'substantive and structural changes' to existing arrangements.[52] It also emphasised the critical role of Emergency Management Australia in preparing for and responding to natural disasters.[53]

Another key issue flagged by the Royal Commission was the need to improve existing arrangements relating to the call-out of the defence forces in emergencies.[54] In September 2020, the Commonwealth pre-empted this recommendation by introducing amendments to its defence legislation, intended to 'streamline' the process for deploying reservists in the event of a large-scale natural disaster or other emergency.[55] These amendments enable the Defence Minister to authorise defence force assistance where 'the nature or scale of the natural disaster or other emergency makes it necessary, for the benefit of the nation'.[56] Michael Head, in commentary upon earlier enactments that confer broad call-out powers in the context of terrorism, has expressed concerns about the breadth of such powers, and the potential for their exercise in quelling civil unrest.[57] Similar issues have been raised in relation to the 2020 Act,[58] in which the term 'emergency' is not defined. The legislation was passed by Parliament in early December.

States of emergency and the pandemic

As health and medical organisations made clear, the megafires constituted a grave threat to public health. In December 2019, 28 groups, including the Royal Australasian College of Physicians and the Public Health Association of Australia, issued a statement in which they described air pollution from the fires in New South Wales as a public health emergency, acknowledged climate change as a causal factor, and called on all levels of government to take urgent measures to reduce greenhouse gas emissions.[59] No such urgent measures were implemented. All levels of government, however, including the federal government, were prepared to respond swiftly and proactively to quite a different public health emergency, following the characterisation of COVID-19 as a pandemic by the World Health Organisation on 11 March 2020.

There is specific legislative provision, in the *Biosecurity Act 2015* (Cth), for the Commonwealth government to declare an emergency in the event of a pandemic. Pursuant to this Act, the Governor-General declared a human biosecurity emergency period for three months from 18 March 2020;[60] this was subsequently extended for additional three-month periods. The federal Minister for Health was thereby empowered to exercise emergency powers under the legislation.[61] State and Territory governments also declared states of emergency under both public health and emergency legislation.[62] In addition, the States and Territories enacted legislation to address the specific public health emergency of the pandemic.[63] Commonwealth, State and

Territory governments coordinated their response to the crisis through the newly established National Cabinet, which met regularly; this was in contrast to the lack of coordinated national response during Black Summer, when the Prime Minister resisted calls for a meeting of the Council of Australian Governments.[64]

These various measures conferred sweeping executive powers[65] and permitted the imposition of significant restrictions. Some commentators have read the response to the pandemic as an expression of transformative possibilities, an exemplary demonstration of how the global community can rapidly and decisively address a planetary emergency. At the outset of the pandemic, novelist Arundhati Roy described it as 'a portal, a gateway between one world and the next', offering 'a chance to rethink the doomsday machine we have built for ourselves'.[66] Writer Roy Scranton hypothesised that the virus might enable us 'to really understand and internalize the fragility and transience of our collective existence'.[67] In his 2020 book *The Climate Cure*, scientist Tim Flannery maintained that, by '[c]ombatting the virus, we have learned how science-based action can lead us out of a crisis'.[68] Swedish scholar Andreas Malm argued that the chronic climate emergency can only be addressed by a form of 'ecological war communism',[69] distinguished by State imposition of 'draconian restraints and cuts'[70] akin to the 'meteor of state interventions that hit the planet in March 2020'.[71]

Other thinkers and commentators were more preoccupied with the immediate and long-term significance of the incursion into individual freedoms and rights. Although similar executive powers were exercised in both Black Summer and during the pandemic, the short-lived curtailment of certain rights and freedoms in response to the megafires passed without question and challenge. The multiple impacts on human rights of the expansion of executive powers during the pandemic became, on the other hand, the focus of intense discussion.[72] Prominent human rights advocates such as expatriate barrister Geoffrey Robertson[73] and President of the Australian Human Rights Commission Rosalind Croucher[74] weighed in on the debate in Australia. Legal challenges to particular pandemic restrictions were mounted.

Widespread restrictions experienced as a consequence of the pandemic provide us with a preview of what lies ahead. Experts consider that future, equally if not more catastrophic climate disasters are unavoidable. On the first day of the Natural Disasters Royal Commission hearings, the Head of Climate Monitoring at the Bureau of Meteorology cautioned that the megafires were not a 'one-off event'.[75] In their final Report, the Commissioners stated that Black Summer 'provided only a glimpse of the types of events that Australia may face in the future'.[76] The Bureau of Meteorology and CSIRO in their 2020 *State of the Climate* report note the long-term, continuing exacerbation of extreme fire weather conditions in Australia as a consequence of climate change.[77] Future climate disasters will occur with increasing frequency; these will, inevitably, usher in further states of emergency and consequential curtailment of rights.

In the following section, I expand upon the exercise of extraordinary executive powers in Australia throughout 2020, and the significance of resulting infringements of our rights and freedoms.

Human rights in a time of fire and plague

At the outset of the pandemic, Giorgio Agamben described emergency measures as 'frenetic, irrational and entirely unfounded'; the 'serious limitations of freedom' amounted to an 'authentic state of exception'. He wrote that '[i]t is almost as if with terrorism exhausted as a cause for exceptional measures, the invention of an epidemic offered the ideal pretext for scaling them up beyond any limitation'.[78] Although other theorists took issue with his position,[79] there is no doubt that the pandemic exposed the precarity of the human rights edifice. This was not merely a matter of philosophical or theoretical concern, as is clear from the numerous anti-lockdown protests against pandemic restrictions. In fact, Sarah Joseph has suggested that human rights may have become somewhat discredited during the pandemic, given the use of rights arguments to support resistance to public health measures.[80]

Under international law, States can disregard certain rights in times of emergency. In one of the key international instruments on human rights, the *International Covenant on Civil and Political Rights*, it is acknowledged that State Parties can, in times of public emergency, adopt measures that derogate from certain of their obligations under the Convention.[81] During the pandemic, however, the United Nations Human Rights Committee cautioned States against doing so beyond the extent strictly required by the exigencies of the public health situation. The Committee stated that 'the predominant objective must be the restoration of a state of normalcy'.[82] A United Nations policy brief on human rights and COVID-19, released in April 2020, emphasised that this was not the time to neglect human rights; rather, the protection of human rights should be a cornerstone of the global response.[83]

Australians, together with many others across the world, were subjected to wide-ranging behavioural restrictions and rights abridgments. Onerous travel bans prevented them from moving freely between continents and States; caps on international arrivals delayed and even blocked the return of Australians to Australia. Upon arrival, travellers were subjected to arbitrary detention in quarantine hotels for a two-week period. In some instances, most notably in Melbourne during a Stage 4 lockdown, freedom of movement was restricted within neighbourhoods. In Western Australia, mobility restrictions could be enforced through the attachment of electronic monitoring devices.[84]

A wide array of rights, in addition to rights of freedom of movement, association and assembly, were impacted; these included rights to work, adequate standards of living, education and a fair trial.[85] As criminologist Alison Young observed, any street could be converted into a crime scene by a police officer exercising their considerable discretion.[86] A group of researchers found early evidence of the intensified use of 'long-standing coercive police tools including stop, search and questioning, arrest and fines and their punitive effects',[87] with a disproportionate impact on First Nations people.[88] Homes, also, were permeable to the police in hitherto unprecedented ways; rights to privacy, family and home came under threat. Ironically, although the measures were designed to protect rights to life and health, the same rights were adversely impacted with, for instance, an exacerbation of mental health problems.[89]

Particular human rights concerns were raised in early July when the Victorian government imposed an immediate hard lockdown, without notice, on 3,000 vulnerable, public housing tower residents; compliance was ensured by a strong police presence.[90] Both federal and Victorian governments maintained that the restrictions were necessary and proportionate. The lockdown, described by a Greens politician as 'dystopian',[91] was subsequently investigated by the Victorian Ombudsman. She concluded that the hasty imposition of the lockdown was incompatible with the residents' human rights, including the right to humane treatment when deprived of liberty.[92] In March 2021, residents filed a class action for damages against the Victorian government.

At the beginning of August, as Victorian cases continued to escalate, the Victorian Premier declared a state of disaster[93] and introduced Stage 4 restrictions, including a controversial night curfew; one commentator described the new measures as analogous to 'martial law in authoritarian regimes'.[94] The three-month lockdown that followed was, at the time, one of the longest in the world.

The extent to which such emergency measures are susceptible to legal challenge was unclear. In New Zealand, faced with a challenge to the government's 'hard' lockdown measures, the High Court took a firm stance. The Court held that the rule of law still mattered in times of emergency, 'even when the merits of the Government response are not widely contested';[95] at such times, 'the courts' constitutional role in keeping a weather eye on the rule of law assumes particular importance'.[96] In an earlier New Zealand lawsuit,[97] arguments of unlawful detention during the hard lockdown had been dismissed.

A number of legal challenges to Victorian restrictions were mounted in 2020.[98] In early November, Justice Ginnane of the Victorian Supreme

Court dismissed a challenge to the night curfew. Acknowledging that '[n]o instance of a curfew being imposed in Victoria by the Executive exists in living memory',[99] he nevertheless held that the power to order a curfew across much of Victoria did exist in a state of emergency,[100] that it was not unreasonable to make the direction,[101] and that the limitations and restrictions on human rights, most notably the right to freedom of movement, were 'proportionate to the purpose of protecting public health'.[102] An attempt to invalidate various directions, including that which confined Melbourne residents to an area within five kilometres of their homes, was also unsuccessful. The High Court dismissed this challenge on the basis that there was no implied constitutional right to freedom of movement.[103]

Federal regulatory measures were the subject of separate challenges. One such lawsuit, commenced in December 2020 by a right-wing think tank, was directed towards the travel ban that prevented citizens from leaving Australia.[104] In March 2021, a group called StrandedAussies.org filed a petition with the United Nations Human Rights Committee, claiming that their right to return to their homeland under the *International Covenant on Civil and Political Rights*[105] was abridged by the Australian government's restrictions on international arrivals.[106]

An additional point of legal contention in Australia concerned State border closures. When the State of Western Australia refused entry to billionaire Clive Palmer, he instigated a lawsuit on the basis that the closures unreasonably limited the constitutionally entrenched freedom of intercourse.[107] The High Court found against him in November, with the five judges handing down their judgments in February 2021.[108] All five judges held that the relevant sections[109] of the *Emergency Management Act 2005* (WA), pursuant to which border closure directions had been made by the State Emergency Coordinator, were valid. In determining the validity of these legislative sections, they drew attention to the temporal restrictions on declared states of emergency, and the statutory requirement that the Minister for Emergency Services must be satisfied of the occurrence or imminence of an emergency, and the need for extraordinary measures.[110] These were, in Justice Gageler's words, 'critical constraints',[111] which ensured that 'the differential burden' on interstate intercourse met 'the requisite standard of reasonable necessity'.[112] Justice Edelman, however, emphasised that not every hypothetical application of these emergency powers would be constitutionally valid.[113]

The High Court's decision to uphold the legitimacy of State border closures, as an extraordinary measure imposed during a state of emergency, raises important questions about cross-border mobility during a climate disaster, and climate mobility within Australia generally. The Natural Disasters Royal Commission emphasised the importance of 'cooperation and coordination' between State governments in 'planning cross border evacuations', during a natural disaster such as the Black Summer megafires.[114] Yet it is relatively easy to imagine permanent State border closures in response to growing numbers of internal climate refugees. Such a scenario, in fact, appears in Alice Robinson's futuristic *The Glad Shout*, in which Tasmania, as a 'safe haven',[115] has 'militarised',[116] with 'tough border control policies' to 'keep it from being inundated'[117] by desperate mainlanders. Future border closures, as the chronic climate emergency intensifies, could well meet the 'requisite standard of reasonable necessity' despite dire consequences for interstate movement.

Anomalies with respect to the implementation of State border closures highlighted another point of convergence between the climate emergency and the pandemic emergency. Both Queensland and Western Australia, at least initially, permitted mine workers who resided in other States to travel freely back and forth across their closed borders.[118] These exemptions indicated that certain corporate activities, and specifically mining projects, were protected from interference during the pandemic, even as human rights were curtailed or set aside for the duration.

Corporate rights during the pandemic

The pandemic, and the initial global response, had a dramatic impact upon the ever-expanding behemoth of global capitalism. Prominent theorist Bruno Latour pointed out that 'we have actually proven that it is possible, in a few weeks, to put an economic system on hold everywhere in the world and at the same time, a system that we were told it was impossible to slow down or redirect'.[119] The pandemic response made abundantly clear the hitherto unacknowledged power of the State to curb economic growth. As Latour put it, resorting to colourful metaphor, 'there was, hidden from us all, a bright red alarm button with a nice big stainless-steel handle that the heads of state could pull, one after the other, to instantly stop the "train of progress" with all the brakes squealing'.[120]

Admittedly, that handle could be pulled only in an emergency. Yet, as many commentators and activists continued to point out throughout the year, the global emergency triggered by COVID-19 was no more urgent or compelling than the climate emergency, and arguably less so.

In Australia, the 'train of progress' was by no means derailed. Prime Minister Morrison's mid-January statement that 'Australia is open for business',[121] intended to reassure international tourists deterred by the dangers and obstacles to safe travel during Black Summer, also captured the approach of both federal and State governments throughout the pandemic. Under the cover of this new emergency, and in some instances using the emergency as a rationale, both levels of governments approved new projects, including mining projects,[122] with little fanfare.

Far from reining in the juggernaut of global capitalism, Australian governments appeared keen to eradicate all existing impediments to development and ongoing extraction of natural resources. The federal government announced its intention to remove 'green tape' from the assessment of major projects.[123] After amending its planning legislation to enable the Minister to unilaterally authorise any development,[124] the New South Wales government introduced an accelerated assessment process to 'get shovel-ready projects out the door'.[125] In the second half of 2020, the New South Wales government approved four major fossil fuel projects.[126] Logging resumed, controversially, in unburnt areas.[127]

It seemed that maintaining a delicate balance between public health concerns and a flourishing economy was germane to governmental decisions on when, and how, to lift restrictions. In the construction of a political hierarchy of emergencies, priority was accorded to the pandemic and a looming recession. At the same time, it became increasingly evident that emergencies were not confined to short-term phenomena capable of definitive resolution.

A hierarchy of emergencies

In September 2020, Greta Thunberg, who shot to global prominence after her first, solitary, school climate strike in 2018, wrote on Twitter that reporting climate disasters and 'connecting the dots' was insufficient; it was imperative that the climate emergency become 'the main focus', that it 'dominate the news', 'all the time'.[128] And yet, in a year of competing emergencies, the climate emergency largely faded into the background.

As flagged in the previous chapter, a recurrent theme in this book is the concept of scalar framing. In the ranking of emergencies, scalar framing comes into play. To deploy the terminology of Dipesh Chakrabarty, we zoom in when it comes to emergencies; the immediate, felt emergency takes precedence over distant emergencies. Distant emergencies, including immense, planetary emergencies that present an existential crisis to humanity, require us to zoom out – a far more challenging and, it would appear, counter-intuitive intellectual exercise.

For Danielle Celermajer, Black Summer 'offered up a rich array of Petri dishes for observing how we, human animals, respond to danger – both the immediate danger of fires approaching, and the other longer-term dangers that they signify'.[129] Millions of Australians, exposed to the dangers of flames and smoke, experienced the climate emergency as lived, immediate reality. The fires seemed never-ending, and yet Black Summer had clear temporal boundaries, a definitive beginning and an end. In its aftermath, the climate emergency receded from media platforms and public debate. The pandemic dominated headlines and shaped government policy, even as the United States West Coast wildfires later in the year, and a sequence of other 'natural' phenomena, served as reminders of the magnitude of the planetary climate crisis.

2020 was also a year in which particular forms of intra-species injustice commanded the public's attention. The Black Lives Matter movement intersected with the pandemic emergency, as thousands of people defied public health warnings in order to engage in mass protests. The interconnection between the climate emergency, the pandemic emergency and the emergency of racial injustice was clear to some; writing on the challenges of 2020, historian Tom Griffiths observed that '[f]ire, plague and racism are always with us, percolating away, periodically erupting, sometimes converging'.[130] For others, however, the emergencies were distinct phenomena and, faced with the simultaneous eruption of multiple emergencies, they typically addressed the most visible or immediate threat. A working hierarchy of emergencies became difficult to sustain as emergencies proliferated and interacted; this was reflected in the IPSOS Issues Monitor Survey, which revealed the fluctuations in the predominant concerns of Australians throughout 2020.[131]

A hierarchy of risk

It is unsurprising, given the tendency to rank multiple emergencies in accordance with perceived risk, that Australia adopts a hierarchical approach in its emergency response system. In the wake of the 2009 Victorian Black Saturday fires, a system of three bushfire alerts, with accompanying icons, was introduced in all States and Territories. This graded system supposedly enabled widespread dissemination of expert assessment of risk for individuals and communities, ranging from the least imperative, 'Advice', to the ambiguous 'Watch and Act' and, at the apex, the Emergency Warning. During Black Summer, the content of emergency warnings was clear: 'You are in danger. Act now to protect yourself. It is too late to leave. The safest option is to take shelter indoors immediately'.[132] The inadequacies of the system became apparent, however, when communications systems failed,[133] fires spread too rapidly for warnings to be updated, and confused residents attempted to make sense of the inherently contradictory statement: Watch and Act. According to journalist Bronwyn Alcock, '[o]n the ground it felt as if we were flying blind'.[134]

Watch and Act alerts, as the Director of Communications of the New South Wales Rural Fire Service conceded while giving evidence at the Royal Commission, generated a 'fair degree of confusion within the community'.[135] Both monitoring in place and evacuation strategies are encompassed in the instruction 'Watch and Act', and this left residents in bushfire-affected areas with a potentially life-threatening dilemma: stay and monitor, or leave while they could. Responsibility for their own safety devolved upon individuals. Furthermore, the warning system was particularly misleading when orchestrated by over-stretched government agencies in overwhelming circumstances. To compound the confusion, some people simultaneously received both Watch and Act, and Emergency Warnings.[136]

Governmental agencies, faced with a growing plenitude of climate catastrophes, are currently revising national warning systems. Commissioner Annabelle Bennett, confronted with an expected delay in the implementation of a revised system, expressed incredulity that the framing of 'three sets of words' could take a projected six or seven years.[137] The imperative for an expeditious rolling out of the Australian Warning System and an updated Australian Fire Danger Rating System was emphasised in the interim report of the Senate inquiry,[138] the report of the Natural Disasters Royal Commission,[139] and the final report of the New South Wales Bushfire Inquiry.[140] A national warning system with three new icons was, in fact, finalised by the end of 2020 but, anomalously, the wording of the 'Watch and Act' warning remained unchanged.[141]

Responding to chronic emergency[142]

Graded warning systems, with emergency alerts that are issued for specific locations and then withdrawn as the risk recedes, reflect the common understanding of emergency: that it is short-lived, immediate and obvious. The goal of emergency governance in the liberal order is 'to drain an event of its eventfulness, making it into a recognized, completed happening and bringing the potentiality that the term emergency gestures towards to an end'.[143] This does not sit well with the chronic climate emergency; it was also, as became increasingly apparent throughout 2020, not readily achievable in the context of the pandemic.

For many Australians, it was only when Victoria experienced a second wave of cases in July that the true nature of the pandemic emergency revealed itself: this emergency, with its accompanying disruptions, was not going to be a short-lived phenomenon. As one journalist put it, there was no 'neat narrative arc with a dramatic beginning and swift resolution'.[144] In a similar vein, novelist John Birmingham mused that the 'metastasising ironies'[145] of 2020 constituted a cautionary lesson against 'narrative complacency'.[146]

The difficulties in adjusting to this realisation[147] provide insight into the framing of the fires as a (relatively) short-term emergency, one which ended with the arrival of heavy rains in February. It was a far more daunting prospect to view the fires, rather, as both part of and symptomatic of a chronic, accelerating, climate emergency. The first Australian bushfire of the 2020 season, in the Tweed Valley in late August, was a sobering reminder that climate and pandemic emergencies could manifest simultaneously; the intersection of such emergencies was more graphically illustrated during the unprecedented fire season in the United States, in the second half of 2020.

In her debut novel *The Inland Sea,*[148] released in Australia at the end of Black Summer, Madeleine Watts addresses the ubiquitous and all-encompassing nature of emergency, and the illusion of personal safety in the face of this. Her narrator, confronted with a broad range of natural disasters and personal crises in her role as Emergency Services Answer Point Representative in a Sydney emergency call centre, finds that the barrier between herself and the external world, with its multiple, unpredictable dangers, has dissolved: '[t]he environment was merely the outer equivalent of my inner reality. Or perhaps it was the other way around'.[149] For many callers to the centre, as for many affected by the Black Summer megafires who were told '[i]f you call for help, you may not get it',[150] assistance is not forthcoming, or arrives too late.[151] They are forced to make their own decisions, to weigh up competing priorities, to save themselves and what can be saved.

The experience of a climate-triggered emergency, such as the megafires, can stimulate survivalist reasoning and foster an individualistic or localised adaptive approach. This approach resonates with the Australian government's emphasis on adaptation and resilience[152] in the wake of the megafires. The Natural Disasters Royal Commission identified the need to foster individual resilience,[153] in conjunction with heightened responsibilities on the part of all levels of government. The resilience 'trope', as Lesley Head has pointed out, is connected in Australia to 'national myths of white survival in a fickle land'.[154] Yet, problematically, a focus upon self-preservation and adaptation can exacerbate fundamental inequalities in the ways in which the climate emergency is and will be experienced, and divert attention away from the global imperative for climate mitigation.

A 'bunker' mentality is not necessarily a byproduct of direct experience of climate emergency.[155] In the wake of a climate disaster, it does seem, however, that those with resources will channel them into shoring up their personal defences. Daniel Aldana Cohen documented the spread of a culture of 'adaptation-focused defensive parochialism'[156] in New York City in the wake of Hurricane Sandy in 2012, and a reduced focus on 'attacking root causes' through decarbonisation.[157] He termed this '"fortress of solitude" social logic'[158] and expressed concern about 'an urban world that looks like a series of fortresses of solitude',[159] in a future with increasingly frequent, extreme weather disasters. The term 'fortress' also appears in Beth Hill's study[160] of the responses of the Blue Mountains community to the Red October fires of 2013. After the fires, survivors constructed improved, more fire-resistant homes. According to Hill, the appearance of these 'bushfire fortresses'[161] represented 'an attempt to shield people both materially and symbolically from the fierce and unstable world of bushfire and its attendant mortality message, and from the shadowy prospect of a climate change'.[162]

It is impossible, concludes Madeleine Watts's narrator, as she engages in increasingly self-destructive, risk-taking behaviour, to protect ourselves from external dangers: '[e]mergency would come for you no matter what you did'.[163] Yet, ultimately, she has saved enough money to flee the 'drought-ridden ancientness'[164] of Australia: an easily contrived departure in the pre-pandemic world, in which the only impediment to global mobility for white Australians was financial.

For privileged groups accustomed to viewing emergency as exceptional, 2020 brought a new appreciation of chronic emergency, alternatively characterised as slow emergency,[165] from which there is no prospect of future relief, no 'anticipatory temporality'.[166] The long-term implications of chronic emergency for the durability of democratic freedoms and democratic systems of governance remained unclear.

Democracy and emergency

Political theorists have wrestled for some decades with the question of whether liberal democracies are the optimal system of governance in an ecological crisis.[167] A number of commentators, including Tim Flannery[168] and science historians Naomi Oreskes and Erik M Conway,[169] have suggested that a state of exception, or some form of authoritarian governance, is required for effective climate mitigation. In a 2019 report, Philip Alston, United Nations Special Rapporteur on Poverty and Human Rights, observed that climate change poses a threat to 'democracy and the rule of law, as well as a wide range of civil and political rights', and speculated that 'States may very well respond to climate change by augmenting government powers and circumscribing some rights'.[170]

Some theorists, however, attempt to reconcile emergency and democracy. Bonnie Honnig argues that emergency and democracy are not incompatible;[171] in Chapter 4, I draw upon her work in my analysis of the use of the extraordinary emergency defence by climate activists. Robyn Eckersley has considered ways in which the challenges of the Anthropocene, including the climate emergency, can be addressed through democratic means, proposing a form of 'geopolitan' or 'down-to-Earth' democracy 'which seeks to build enhanced reflexivity from the bottom up'.[172]

Furthermore, current social movements emphasise the importance of democratic mechanisms in addressing the climate crisis. Citizen participation is integral to the youth climate strike movement; in an open letter sent to all European heads of state in July 2020, four youth climate leaders included the safeguarding and protection of democracy in their list of demands.[173] Extinction Rebellion agitates for the establishment of citizens' assemblies to guide governments in their response to the climate emergency. In this, the movement is drawing upon a growing number of such experiments in deliberative democracy.

One such example is the Irish citizens' assembly, established in 2016 with the remit of addressing five public policy issues, including the climate crisis.[174] The assembly's recommendations influenced the development of a 2019 Climate Action Plan.[175] A more recent exemplar of a climate citizens' assembly is the Convention Citoyenne pour le Climat, established by French President Macron in 2019. The convention consisted of randomly selected French citizens, drawn by lot and tasked with finding ways to reduce greenhouse gas emissions within a social justice framework. It submitted 149 findings to the French President in June 2020, including a recommendation for the recognition, in French law, of the crime of ecocide.

Another climate citizens' assembly was established in the United Kingdom in June 2019, and reported to the British government in September 2020. Its role was to identify avenues for achieving a net zero emissions target by 2050, a goal at odds with the Extinction Rebellion demand for a net zero target by 2025; furthermore, aviation, trade and international emissions were not factored into the assembly's calculations.[176] A Scottish Climate Assembly held its first meeting in November 2020.

Although citizens' assemblies have some fundamental shortcomings,[177] the importance of these initiatives cannot be overstated. This is particularly so in light of the vulnerability of democratic freedoms in states of exception. Citizens' assemblies enable and legitimise popular engagement in decision-making on the climate emergency. Danielle Celermajer and Dalia Nassar contend that 'political communities that are well practiced in the arts of solidaristic collective action' will be 'best equipped to offer more-than-totalitarian responses to disasters'.[178]

One important concern is that the viewpoint presented in these citizens' assemblies, which are designed to be representative of the broader population in terms of demographics,[179] may not reflect the disproportionate impact of the climate emergency upon Indigenous people. In the words of two commentators, such representative assemblies may 'perpetuate a form of climate and ecological "justice" that continues to privilege whiteness/maintain white supremacy'.[180] In the following sections, I consider Indigenous narratives of emergency in the Australian context, and acknowledge the ways in which the megafires, and the climate emergency generally, have affected and will affect Indigenous people.

Indigenous narratives of emergency

Privileged classes may well view states of exception, and indeed apocalypse, as yet to come. Nevertheless, countless numbers of people have lived through past, 'localized' apocalypses;[181] Mark O'Connell observes that '[i]t was always the end of the world for someone, somewhere'.[182] Other incalculable numbers are enduring contemporary versions of apocalypse. This stark reality can sometimes be disregarded by those reflecting upon climate change as an existential crisis; in a review of a 2020 collection of essays on the Anthropocene, Prithvi Varatharajan noted a misleading reference to a 'univeralised "we"' confronting extinction for the 'first time in history'.[183]

As one group of researchers has observed, the 'promise and hope' that 'the everyday or ordinary can be separated from emergency/disaster' was 'only ever available to certain valued lives'.[184] For Aboriginal people, living through a state of emergency as 'bare life' is not a new experience; it has been their lived experience of colonisation for generations. Claire Coleman, Indigenous writer of speculative fiction, has commented that 'Aboriginal people live in a dystopia every day'[185] and conveys this everyday reality, and the apocalyptic nature of the colonisation process, in her allegorical novel *Terra Nullius*. The reader belatedly realises that the violence of colonisation is, in this fictitious context, a universal experience for humanity; alien 'Settlers' have invaded Earth, and dispossessed and enslaved all human inhabitants.

Indigenous academics Megan Davis and Nicole Watson have pointed out that 'the history of the curtailment of Indigenous freedoms in Australia' makes it very clear that Australian Parliaments are 'well rehearsed in limiting the exercise of fundamental rights'.[186] Victoria Grieves argues that Aboriginal people reside in a state of exception,[187] and suggests that they are 'truly *homo sacer*':[188] humans without rights. Melissa Lucashenko, writing about the impact of the pandemic on Indigenous people in Australia, has put it thus:

> Well, here's the thing. When you are Indigenous, and when you live as colonised Indigenous people for generations, your mob learns certain things. About exclusion, for instance, and the meaning of marginalisation. About how to distinguish necessity from luxury, and truth from lies. About how to survive generation after generation of externally imposed hard times.[189]

There is nothing remotely new for Aboriginal people in living through and enduring a chronic state of emergency, or state of exception, nor in being denied fundamental rights. Lockdowns are neither novel nor unprecedented.

Forced removal from Country has been an ongoing feature of colonisation. Indigenous people are accustomed to watching, without being able to intervene, as their children's future is compromised and their opportunities diminished; this has been described in the historic *Uluru Statement from the Heart* as 'the torment of our powerlessness'.[190]

Thus, much of the preceding discussion concerning the limited comprehension of the nature of chronic emergencies, and the widespread reluctance to accept necessary sacrifices that must occur in response to such emergencies, reflects the viewpoint of white privilege. This observation is not intended to downplay the impact of the climate emergency on Indigenous people. Remote settlements in areas of Australia may well become uninhabitable due to extreme heat. Furthermore, a 2019 complaint against the Morrison government, brought by eight Torres Strait Islander people before the United Nations Human Rights Committee,[191] brings into sharp relief the existential dangers and human rights violations faced by the Islanders as a consequence of sea level rise.

In the *Mabo* case, in which the High Court recognised the connection to land and native title rights of the Torres Strait Islanders, Justice Brennan famously stated that 'when the tide of history has washed away any real acknowledgment of traditional law and any real observance of traditional customs, the foundation of native title has disappeared'.[192] The Islanders now confront 'the total submergence of ancestral homelands' and 'violation of the rights to culture, family and life',[193] as a consequence of the tides of climate change. In August 2020, the government asked the Commission to dismiss the complaint, on the basis that Australia is not the only nation responsible for rising emissions and climate impacts and that, furthermore, the alleged impacts and human rights violations have not yet occurred.[194]

Connection to Country and the megafires

In the aftermath of the fires, there has been a growing interest in traditional Indigenous methods of land management through cultural burning. Custodians of these techniques such as Victor Steffensen, whose book *Fire Country*[195] was released in 2020, are running workshops and assisting property owners with fire prevention techniques. Less attention has been directed towards the experiences of Indigenous people directly affected by the megafires.[196]

Researchers have noted the disproportionate representation of Indigenous people in the fire-affected areas of NSW and Victoria,[197] and the disproportionate effects upon Indigenous children.[198] The megafires, as an aspect of the climate emergency, had a devastating impact upon Aboriginal people, destroying or endangering countless aspects of their cultural heritage and jeopardising their connection to Country. Bhiamie Williamson, giving evidence at the Natural Disasters Royal Commission, pointed out that:

> The impact of disasters such as the bushfires disrupts the attachment to lands and waters and deeply impacts the existence of Aboriginal peoples. Indeed, the destruction of landscape features, whether that be plant species, native animals or cultural heritage sites such as scar trees, rock art or stone arrangements, threatens Aboriginal groups as distinct cultural beings attached to the land.[199]

During the fires, and in their aftermath, Aboriginal people articulated a profound sense of grief and loss. Gabrielle Fletcher, a Gundungurra woman from the Blue Mountains of New South Wales, alluded to a communal sense of 'irresponsible helplessness' in being forced to abandon obligations of caring for Country.[200] Paola Balla, together with other Aboriginal writers, viewed the 'ecocidal fire storms' as a continuation of fires used as part of the colonisation process, stating that '[w]e are burnt out yet again'. She contemplated the permanent loss of Country with despair and foreboding: 'Perhaps, as some Mob have said, the Country is *beyond healing*, beyond being able to be cared for properly again. This is a desecration of all that we as Aboriginal Peoples hold sacred'.[201] Reflecting upon the consequences of the 'worst bushfires in our history', Warren Foster, a Yuin man from Wallaga Lake in the south coast of New South Wales, explained that '[w]e need our country to be healthy so we can be healthy'.[202] Lorena Allam, a Yuin woman, has described the 'particular grief' of 'los[ing] forever what connects you to a place in the landscape'.[203]

In the aftermath of the megafires, and in light of the looming threat of future conflagrations, both Aboriginal and non-Aboriginal people confront the prospect of permanent displacement and relocation as fire or climate refugees. This scenario, however, has complex ramifications for Aboriginal people, for whom being on Country involves far more than the exercise of property rights.[204] They face, as Lorena Allam puts it, 'lifelong double dislocation'.[205]

For a people whose system of raw law[206] is so intimately connected to Country, the ravages of the megafires were catastrophic on a number of levels, not least by the contribution of the megafires in pushing certain species to the brink of extinction. Deborah Bird Rose has observed that 'Country is not just the homeland for humans, but the homeland for all the living things that are there, and care is circulated through country in cross-species relationships of responsibility and accountability'.[207] The strong, cross-species, kinship connections between Aboriginal people and nonhuman beings are severed by extinctions.[208]

Conclusion

As I have shown here, emergency discourses became prevalent, almost commonplace, in 2020. I have suggested that the construction of a hierarchy of emergencies enabled vastly inconsistent responses: the global emergency of the pandemic, and its accompanying economic recession, prompted swift governmental intervention while the climate emergency, despite the galvanising impact of the megafires of Black Summer, remained a secondary concern for Australian and other governments.

Nevertheless, the emergency response to the pandemic contains many valuable lessons as to how drastic responses to the climate emergency can be shaped, and directed, in the future. It highlights the vulnerability of our rights and freedoms, and our democratic systems of governance, in states of emergency.

I have outlined some of the fundamental inequities and injustices in the ways in which particular groups experience emergency, exemplified in the uniquely catastrophic effects of the megafires upon Aboriginal people and their relationship with Country. During 2020, an additional emergency narrative dominated public debate: the global narrative of racial injustice, which in Australia constitutes part of the 'long transitive moment'[209] of the chronic emergency of colonisation. 2020 has been described as a year of 'crisis conglomeration',[210] featuring an 'overlapping sequence of horrors',[211] but the indiscriminate and relentless nature of its cascading panoply of emergencies was a novel experience only for privileged, white citizens of the Global North. For marginalised groups in various parts of the world, including in Australia, there is nothing remarkable about existing within the restrictive parameters of ongoing states of emergency.

The relentless cycle of black deaths in custody in Australia, notwithstanding wide-ranging recommendations handed down by a Royal Commission into Aboriginal Deaths in Custody in 1991, was labelled a national emergency by the National Aboriginal and Torres Strait Islander Legal Service;[212] between June and September 2020 alone, five such deaths occurred. In Chapter 4, I consider the Black Lives Matter movement as another emergency discourse performed in the zealously policed and surveilled public spaces of the pandemic.

In Chapter 4, I also analyse the emergency narrative presented by some Australian climate activists during their 2020 trials. Importantly, in both public spaces and courtrooms, such popular invocations disentangle the discourse of emergency from the states of exception engendered by executive declaration.

Notes

1 Fiona Harvey and Jillian Ambrose, 'Pope Francis Declares "Climate Emergency" and Urges Action', *The Guardian* (online, 15 June 2019) <www.theguardian.com/environment/2019/jun/14/pope-francis-declares-climate-emergency-and-urges-action>.

2 William J Ripple et al, “World Scientists Warning of a Climate Emergency” (2020) 70(1) *Bioscience* 8.

3 Will Steffen et al, ‘The Trajectory of the Anthropocene: The Great Acceleration’ (2015) 2 *The Anthropocene Review* 81.

4 ‘The Safe Climate Declaration’ (National Climate Emergency Summit, 2020) <www.climateemergencysummit.org/declaration>.

5 Patrick Greenfield, ‘World Leaders Pledge to Halt Earth’s Destruction ahead of UN Summit’, *The Guardian* (online, 28 September 2020) <www.theguardian.com/environment/2020/sep/28/world-leaders-pledge-to-halt-earth-destruction-un-summit>.

6 Quoted in Bevan Shields, ‘Every Country Must Declare a State of “Climate Emergency”, UN Chief Tells World Leaders’, *The Sydney Morning Herald* (online, 13 December 2020) <www.smh.com.au/world/europe/every-country-must-declare-a-state-of-climate-emergency-un-chief-tells-world-leaders-20201212-p56mz5.html>.

7 Katharine Murphy, ‘Scott Morrison Refuses to Commit to Net Zero Emissions Target by 2050’, *The Guardian* (online, 20 September 2020) <www.theguardian.com/australia-news/2020/sep/20/scott-morrison-refuses-to-commit-to-net-zero-emissions-target-by-2050>.

8 *Royal Commission into National Natural Disaster Arrangements* (Report, 28 October 2020) 22 (‘Natural Disasters Royal Commission Report’).

9 Jocelyn Stacey, *The Constitution of the Environmental Emergency* (Hart, 2018) 19.

10 Carl Schmitt, *Political Theology: Four Chapters on the Concept of Sovereignty*, tr George Schwab (University of Chicago Press, 2005) 7.

11 Ibid 12.

12 Jenny Hocking, *Terror Laws: ASIO, Counter-Terrorism and the Threat to Democracy* (University of New South Wales Press, 2004) 214.

13 Matthew Sharpe, ‘“Thinking of the Extreme Situation . . .”: On the New Anti-Terrorism Laws or Against a Recent (Theoretical and Legal) Return to Carl Schmitt’ (2006) 24 *Australian Feminist Law Journal* 95, 97.

14 Ibid 101.

15 Giorgio Agamben, *State of Exception*, tr Kevin Attell (University of Chicago Press, 2005) 4.

16 Tom Cohen, ‘The Geomorphic Fold: Anapocalyptics, Changing Climes and “Late” Deconstruction’ (2010) 32(1) *The Oxford Literary Review* 71, 72 (emphasis in original).

17 Bruce Lindsay, ‘Climate of Exception: What Might a “Climate Emergency” Mean in Law?’ (2010) 38 *Federal Law Review* 255, 268 (emphasis in original).

18 Ibid 269.

19 See discussion of Australian civil emergencies and special powers legislation in Hoong Phun Lee, Michael WR Adams, Colin Campbell and Patrick Emerton, *Emergency Powers in Australia* (Cambridge University Press, 2nd ed, 2019) ch 6.

20 Agamben (n 15) 51.

21 Roberto Esposito, *Immunitas: The Protection and Negation of Life*, tr Zakiya Hana (Polity Press, 2011), 8.

22 See Lee et al (n 19) 191.

23 Stacey (n 9) 19.

24 David Dyzenhaus, *The Constitution of Law: Legality in a Time of Emergency* (Cambridge University Press, 2006) 50.

25 Ibid 39.

26 David Dyzenhaus, 'Cycles of Legality in Emergency Times' (2007) 18 *Public Law Review* 165, 168.
27 Ibid 185.
28 'Victorian Fires: State of Disaster Declared as Evacuation Ordered and 28 People Missing', *The Guardian* (online, 3 January 2020) <www.theguardian.com/australia-news/2020/jan/03/victoria-fires-state-of-disaster-declared-as-evacuation-ordered-and-second-man-found-dead>.
29 *State of Emergency and Rescue Management Act 1989* (NSW) ss 37, 37A, 38.
30 *Fire and Emergency Services Act 1990* (Qu) s 89.
31 Ibid s 91.
32 Under *Emergency Management Act 1986* (Vic) s 23.
33 *2009 Victorian Bushfires Royal Commission* (Final Report, July 2010) Summary, 26.
34 *Emergency Management Act 1986* (Vic) s 24(2)(c), (d), (e).
35 Ibid s 24(2)(b).
36 *2009 Victorian Bushfires Royal Commission* (n 33) vol 2, 2.5.1.
37 *Emergencies Act 2004* (ACT) s 156.
38 Ibid s 160A.
39 Lee et al (n 19) 171.
40 Ibid 7.
41 Ibid 171.
42 Natural Disasters Royal Commission Report (n 8) 24.
43 Rob Harris and David Crowe, 'Porter Narrows National Emergency Powers in Peace Deal with Backbench', *The Sydney Morning Herald* (online, 3 December 2020) <www.theage.com.au/politics/federal/porter-narrows-national-mergency-powers-in-peace-deal-with-backbench-20201202-p56k1c.html>.
44 National Emergency Declaration Bill 2020 (Cth) s 11(1)(c)(iv).
45 Ibid s 11(3)(b).
46 The Senate, Finance and Public Administration References Committee, *Lessons to Be Learned in Relation to the Australian Bushfire Season 2019–20* (Interim Report, October 2020) 65 ('Senate Interim Report').
47 Mike Seccombe, 'Bushfire Hearings Spotlight Climate Change' (30 May–5 June 2020) *The Saturday Paper* <www.thesaturdaypaper.com.au/news/politics/2020/05/30/bushfire-hearings-spotlight-climate-change/15907608009902>.
48 Andrew Tillett, 'Army Reservists Begin to Make Their Mark on Fire Recovery', *Financial Review* (online, 6 January 2020) <www.afr.com/politics/federal/army-reservists-begin-to-make-their-mark-on-fire-recovery-20200106-p53p6z>.
49 See, eg, Alan Weedon, 'Scott Morrison Criticised for Running "Absolutely Obscene" Political Ads during Bushfires', *ABC News* (online, 5 January 2020) <www.abc.net.au/news/2020-01-05/scott-morrison-criticised-for-political-ads-during-bushfires/11841458>.
50 'Scott Morrison Heckled after He Tries to Shake Hands with Bushfire Victim in NSW Town of Cobargo', *The Guardian* (online, 2 January 2020) <www.theguardian.com/australia-news/2020/jan/02/scott-morrison-abused-by-bushfire-victims-in-nsw-town-of-cobargo>; Tony Wright, '"He Said What the Rest of Us Were Thinking": Firefighter Who Sprayed PM Sees Free Beers Flow In', *The Age* (online, 14 February 2020) <www.theage.com.au/politics/federal/he-said-what-the-rest-of-us-were-thinking-firefighter-who-sprayed-pm-sees-free-beers-flow-in-20200214-p540rt.html>.

51 Evidence to Royal Commission into National Natural Disaster Arrangements, Canberra, 6 July 2020, 1500 (Greg Mullins); Senate Interim Report (n 46) 57.
52 Natural Disasters Royal Commission Report (n 8) 74.
53 Ibid 27.
54 Ibid 202.
55 Explanatory Memorandum, Defence Legislation Amendment (Enhancement of Defence Force Response to Emergencies) Bill 2020 (Cth).
56 Defence Legislation Amendment (Enhancement of Defence Force Response to Emergencies) Bill 2020 (Cth) sch 2, s 4.
57 Michael Head, 'Another Expansion of Military Call Out Powers in Australia: Some Critical Legal, Constitutional and Political Questions' (2019) No 5 *UNSW Law Journal Forum* 1, 14.
58 See, eg, Commonwealth, *Parliamentary Debates*, House of Representatives, 6 October 2020, 56 (Zali Steggall).
59 'Joint Statement: Air Pollution in NSW Is a Public Health Emergency', *Climate and Health Alliance* (Post, 16 December 2019) <www.caha.org.au/air-pollution>.
60 This was the first time such a declaration had been made under the Act.
61 *Biosecurity Act 2015* (Cth) ss 475–8.
62 Queensland declared a public health emergency under the *Public Health Act 2005* (Qu); South Australia made a declaration of a major emergency under the *Emergency Management Act 2004* (SA); Victoria declared a state of emergency under the *Public Health and Wellbeing Act 2008* (Vic) and subsequently, in August, declared a state of disaster under the *Emergency Management Act 1986* (Vic); Tasmania declared a state of emergency under the *Emergency Management Act 2006* (Tas) and made a public health emergency declaration under the *Public Health Act 1997* (Tas); the Northern Territory declared a public health emergency under the *Public and Environmental Health Act 2011* (NT); Western Australia declared a state of emergency under the *Emergency Management Act 2005* (WA) and a public health state of emergency under the *Public Health Act 2016* (WA); the ACT made a public health (emergency) declaration under the *Public Health Act 1997* (ACT). Under the relevant public health legislation in New South Wales, the *Public Health Act 2010* (NSW), it is not necessary for the State to declare a state of emergency in order to enable the relevant Minister to make orders and declarations (s 7).
63 See, inter alia, *COVID-19 Emergency Response Act 2020* (Qld); *COVID-19 Legislation Amendment (Emergency Measures – Miscellaneous) Act 2020* (NSW); *COVID-19 Emergency Response Act 2020* (SA); *COVID-19 Omnibus (Emergency Measures) Act 2020* (Vic); *COVID-19 Disease Emergency (Miscellaneous Provisions) Act 2020* (Tas); *Emergency Management Amendment (COVID-19 Response) Act 2020* (WA); *COVID-19 Emergency Response Act 2020* (ACT); *Emergency Legislation Amendment Act 2020* (NT).
64 David Crowe, '"Morrison Is Losing Skin": PM Too Passive in the Face of National Crisis', *The Age* (online, 3 January 2020) <www.theage.com.au/national/morrison-is-losing-skin-pm-too-passive-in-the-face-of-national-crisis-20200102-p53odj.html>.
65 For example, under the *Public Health and Other Legislation (Public Health Emergency) Amendment Act 2020* (Qu), the *Public Health Act 2005* (Qu) was amended such that the Queensland Chief Health Officer could make any direction considered necessary to protect public health (*Public Health Act* s 362B(2)(e)).

66 Arundhati Roy, 'The Pandemic Is a Portal', *Financial Times* (online, 4 April 2020) <www.ft.com/content/10d8f5e8-74eb-11ea-95fe-fcd274e920ca>.
67 Roy Scranton, 'I've Said Goodbye to "Normal": You Should, Too', *The New York Times* (online, 25 January 2021) <www.nytimes.com/2021/01/25/opinion/new-normal-climate-catastrophes.html>.
68 Tim Flannery, *The Climate Cure: Solving the Climate Emergency in the Era of COVID-19* (Text Publishing, 2020) 13.
69 Andreas Malm, *Corona, Climate and Chronic Emergency: War Communism in the Twenty-First Century* (Verso, 2020) 167.
70 Ibid 143.
71 Ibid 27.
72 See, eg, articles in a September 2020 special issue of the *Alternative Law Journal* on COVID-19 including Janina Boughey, 'Executive Power in Emergencies: Where Is the Accountability?' (2020) 45(3) *Alternative Law Journal* 168; Kylie Evans and Nicholas Petrie, 'COVID-19 and the Australian Human Rights Acts' (2020) 45(3) *Alternative Law Journal* 175.
73 Bevan Shields, 'Australia's COVID-19 Flight Caps Breach Human Rights: Geoffrey Robertson', *The Sydney Morning Herald* (online, 12 November 2020) <www.smh.com.au/world/europe/australia-s-covid-19-flight-caps-breach-human-rights-geoffrey-robertson-20201107-p56cc8.html>.
74 David Crowe, 'Warning Travel Restrictions Could Breach Human Rights', *The Sydney Morning Herald* (online, 22 October 2020) <www.smh.com.au/politics/federal/warning-travel-restrictions-could-breach-human-rights-20201022-p567qx.html>.
75 Evidence to Royal Commission into National Natural Disaster Arrangements, Canberra, 25 May 2020, 15 (Dr Karl Braganza).
76 Natural Disasters Royal Commission Report (n 8) 22.
77 CSIRO and Australian Government Bureau of Meteorology, *State of the Climate Report* (Report, 2020) 5, 22.
78 Giorgio Agamben, 'The Invention of an Epidemic' (26 February 2020) *Quodlibet* <www.quodlibet.it/giorgio-agamben-l-invenzione-di-un-epidemia>; reproduced in 'Coronavirus and Philosophers' (2020) *European Journal of Psychoanalysis* <www.journal-psychoanalysis.eu/coronavirus-and-philosophers/#_ftn2>.
79 See, eg, commentary by Jean-Luc Nancy, Roberto Esposito and Sergio Benvenuto in 'Coronavirus and Philosophers' (n 78).
80 Sarah Joseph, 'Human Rights and COVID-19' (2020 Alice Tay Lecture on Law and Human Rights, 28 October 2020).
81 *International Covenant on Civil and Political Rights*, opened for signature 19 December 1966, 999 UNTS 171 (entered into force 23 March 1976) Art 4 ('*ICCPR*').
82 Human Rights Committee, 'Statement on Derogations from the Covenant in Connection with the COVID-19 Pandemic', 30 April 2020, CCPR/C/128/2.
83 'COVID-19 and Human Rights: We Are All in This Together' (United Nations Secretary-General's Policy Brief, April 2020) <www.un.org/sites/un2.un.org/files/un_policy_brief_on_human_rights_and_covid_23_april_2020.pdf>.
84 *Emergency Management Act 2005* (WA) s 70A.
85 See Sarah Joseph, 'COVID-19, Risk and Rights: The "Wicked" Balancing Act for Governments', *The Conversation* (online, 16 September 2020) <https://theconversation.com/covid-19-risk-and-rights-the-wicked-balancing-act-for-governments-146014>.

86 Alison Young, 'Crime Scenes in a Ghost Town: The Atmospherics of Lockdown' (Critical Issues Seminar, University of Melbourne, 4 August 2020).

87 Louise Boon-Kuo et al, 'Policing Biosecurity: Police Enforcement of Special Measures in New South Wales and Victoria during the COVID-19 Pandemic' (2020) *Current Issues in Criminal Justice* 1–13, 6 <https://doi.org/10.1080/10345329.2020.1850144>.

88 Ibid 5–6.

89 Joseph (n 80).

90 Ashleigh McMillan, '"It'll Be Five Hard Days": Extreme Lockdown in Melbourne's Public Housing Towers Begins', *The Age* (online, 4 July 2020) <www.theage.com.au/national/victoria/it-ll-be-five-hard-days-extreme-lockdown-in-melbourne-s-public-housing-towers-begins-20200704-p5591r.html>; David Estcourt and Clay Lucas, 'Thousands of Public Housing Tenants under Hard Lockdown as COVID-19 Spreads', *The Age* (online, 4 July 2020) <www.theage.com.au/national/victoria/thousands-of-public-housing-tenants-under-hard-lockdown-as-covid-19-spreads-20200704-p5590s.html>.

91 Quoted in Estcourt and Lucas (n 90).

92 Victorian Ombudsman, *Investigation into the Detention and Treatment of Public Housing Residents Arising from a COVID-19 "Hard Lockdown" in July 2020* (Report, December 2020) 18.

93 Under section 23(1) of the *Emergency Management Act 1986* (Vic), the Premier can declare a state of disaster if satisfied that there is an emergency which constitutes or is likely to constitute a significant and widespread danger to life or property in Victoria.

94 Editorial, 'State of Disaster Resorts to Desperate Covid Measures', *The Australian* (online, 3 August 2020) <www.theaustralian.com.au/commentary/editorials/state-of-disaster-resorts-to-desperate-covid-measures/news-story/72bb5fa3233ed15a5fa9905ec57a838a>.

95 *Borrowdale v Director-General of Health* [2020] NZHC 2090 [2].

96 Ibid [291].

97 *A v Ardern* [2020] NZHC 796 (23 April 2020).

98 David Estcourt, 'The COVID-19 Lawsuits Faced by the Andrews Government', *The Age* (online, 22 October 2020) <www.theage.com.au/national/victoria/the-covid-19-lawsuits-faced-by-the-andrews-government-20201016-p565te.html>.

99 *Loielo v Giles* [2020] VSC 722 [2].

100 Ibid [16].

101 Ibid [20].

102 Ibid [21].

103 *Gerner v Victoria* [2020] HCA 48.

104 Paul Karp, 'Rightwing Thinktank Launches Legal Challenge to Australia's Travel Ban', *The Guardian* (online, 16 December 2020) <www.theguardian.com/australia-news/2020/dec/16/rightwing-thinktank-launches-legal-challenge-to-australias-travel-ban>.

105 *ICCPR* (n 81) Art 12(4).

106 Ellie Dudley, 'Coronavirus Australia: Stranded Aussies File Legal Action with the UN against the Federal Government', *The Australian* (online, 31 March 2021) <www.theaustralian.com.au/nation/coronavirus-australia-stranded-aussies-file-legal-action-with-the-un-against-the-federal-government/news-story/a9d33939ce441dac9fa27592f10d611f>.

107 *Australian Constitution* s 92.
108 *Palmer v Western Australia* [2021] HCA 5. This followed findings of fact handed down by a Federal Court judge in August 2020, in *Palmer v Western Australia [No 4]* [2020] FCA 1221.
109 *Emergency Management Act 2005* (WA) ss 56, 67.
110 *Palmer v Western Australia* [2021] HCA 5 [69]-[70] (Kiefel CJ, Keane J); [77], [156]-[159] (Gageler J); [174]-[175], [206]-[208] (Gordon J); [282]-[284] (Edelman J).
111 Ibid [126] (Gageler J).
112 Ibid [166] (Gageler J).
113 Ibid [227]-[228] (Edelman J).
114 Natural Disasters Royal Commission Report (n 8) 281.
115 Alice Robinson, *The Glad Shout* (Affirm Press, 2019) 171.
116 Ibid 13.
117 Ibid 171–2.
118 Ben Smee, 'Queensland Miners Fear FIFO Workers Could Pose a Threat during Coronavirus Pandemic', *The Guardian* (online, 25 March 2020) <www.theguardian.com/business/2020/mar/25/queensland-miners-fear-fifo-workers-could-pose-a-threat-during-coronavirus-pandemic>; Clint Jasper and Michelle Stanley, 'Coronavirus Threat Prompts Mining Companies to Implement New Procedures to Avoid Outbreaks', *ABC News* (online, 27 March 2020) <www.abc.net.au/news/2020-03-27/coronavirus-mining-and-resources-new-procedures/12062380>.
119 Bruno Latour, 'What Protective Measures Can You Think of So We Don't Go Back to the Pre-Crisis Production Model?', tr Stephen Muecke, *Bruno Latour* (Post, 2020) <www.bruno-latour.fr/sites/default/files/P-202-AOC-ENGLISH.pdf>.
120 Ibid.
121 'Australia "Open for Business", Morrison Tells Tourists', *The Business Times* (online, 15 January 2020) <www.businesstimes.com.sg/government-economy/australia-open-for-business-morrison-tells-tourists>.
122 For instance, the New South Wales government approved a mining project under the Woronora reservoir in March, while Parliament was suspended: Lisa Cox, 'Fears for Water Quality after NSW Allows Coalmining Extension under Sydney's Woronora Reservoir', *The Guardian* (online, 31 March 2020) <www.theguardian.com/environment/2020/mar/31/fears-for-water-quality-after-nsw-allows-coalmining-extension-under-sydneys-worona-reservoir>.
123 Mike Foley, 'More Funding Needed in Government Push to Cut "Green Tape": Industry', *The Sydney Morning Herald* (online, 3 August 2020) <www.smh.com.au/politics/federal/more-funding-needed-in-government-push-to-cut-green-tape-industry-20200730-p55h41.html>.
124 *Environmental Planning and Assessment Act 1979* (NSW) s 10.17, amended under the *COVID-19 Legislation Amendment (Emergency Measures) Act 2020* (NSW) s 2.8.
125 Planning and Public Spaces Minister Rob Stokes, quoted in Angus Thompson, 'The 13 New NSW Projects Set to Inject More Than $4 Billion into the Economy', *The Sydney Morning Herald* (online, 17 July 2020) <www.smh.com.au/national/nsw/the-13-nsw-projects-set-to-inject-more-than-4-billion-into-the-economy-20200717-p55d52.html>.
126 Lisa Cox, 'NSW Independent Planning Commission Accused of Acting as "Rubber Stamp" as Coalmine Approved', *The Guardian* (online, 24 December

2020) <www.theguardian.com/australia-news/2020/dec/24/nsw-independent-planning-commission-accused-of-acting-as-rubber-stamp-as-coalmine-approved>.

127 David Lindenmayer and Doug Robinson, 'Logging is Due to Start in Fire-Ravaged Forests This Week: It's the Last Thing Our Wildlife Needs', *The Conversation* (online, 2 March 2020) <https://theconversation.com/logging-is-due-to-start-in-fire-ravaged-forests-this-week-its-the-lastthing-our-wildlife-needs-132347>; Miki Perkins and Mike Foley, 'Logging Returns to NSW Native Forests Hit by Bushfires', *The Sydney Morning Herald* (online, 1 May 2020) <www.smh.com.au/national/logging-returns-to-native-forests-hit-by-bushfires-20200501-p54ots.html>; Paddy Manning, 'Coupe de Grace' (November 2020) *The Monthly* <www.themonthly.com.au/issue/2020/november/1604149200/paddy-manning/coupe-de-gr-ce>.

128 Louise Boyle, '"Connecting the Dots Is Not Enough": Greta Thunberg Demands That the Climate Crisis "Dominate" News Cycle', *The Independent* (online, 11 September 2020) <www.independent.co.uk/environment/connecting-dots-not-enough-furious-greta-thunberg-b421704.html>.

129 Danielle Celermajer, *Summertime: Reflections on a Vanishing Future* (Hamish Hamilton, 2021) 58–9.

130 Tom Griffiths, 'Drawing Breath' in Sophie Cunningham (ed), *Fire, Flood and Plague: Australian Writers Respond to 2020* (Vintage Books, 2020) 53, 53.

131 Matt Wade, 'Pandemic Fret: Australia's Five Biggest Worries Heading into 2021', *The Age* (online, 11 January 2021) <www.theage.com.au/national/pandemic-fret-australia-s-five-biggest-worries-heading-into-2021-20210110-p56t0j.html>.

132 Quoted in Amy Coopes, 'Dear Australia, Elegy for a Summer of Loss', *The Guardian* (online, 23 January 2020) <www.theguardian.com/commentisfree/2020/jan/23/dear-australia-elegy-for-a-summer-of-loss>.

133 Evidence to Royal Commission into National Natural Disaster Arrangements, Canberra, 22 June 2020, 960–962 (Des Schroder and John McArthur); 1009, 1011, 1013 (Matthew Hyde, Juliana Phelps and Peter Bascomb).

134 Bronwyn Adcock, 'Living Hell' (February 2020) *The Monthly* <www.themonthly.com.au/issue/2020/february/1580475600/bronwyn-adcock/living-hell#mtr>.

135 Evidence to Royal Commission into National Natural Disaster Arrangements, Canberra, 1 July 2020, 1215 (Anthony Clark).

136 Natural Disasters Royal Commission Report (n 8) 296.

137 Royal Commission into National Natural Disaster Arrangements, Canberra, 1 July 2020, 1217 (Commissioner Annabelle Bennett).

138 Senate Interim Report (n 46) 167–8.

139 Natural Disasters Royal Commission Report (n 8) 285, 294, 299.

140 *Final Report of the NSW Bushfire Inquiry* (31 July 2020) 138–9.

141 Declan Gooch, 'Emergency Warnings for Bushfires, Floods and Cyclones about to Get Clearer', *ABC News* (online, 1 December 2020) <www.abc.net.au/news/2020-12-01/bushfire-flood-cyclone-warnings-national-system-clearer/12931450>.

142 The term chronic emergency in the context of the climate crisis is used by Andreas Malm in Malm (n 69).

143 Ben Anderson et al, 'Slow Emergencies: Temporality and the Racialized Biopolitics of Emergency Governance' (2020) 44(4) *Progress in Human Geography* 621, 625.

144 Josephine Tovey, 'The Second Wave: "Thinking This Would End Was a Useful Crutch: Now It's Been Kicked from under Us"', *The Guardian* (online, 9 July 2020) <www.theguardian.com/lifeandstyle/2020/jul/09/the-second-wave-thinking-this-would-end-was-a-useful-crutch-now-its-been-kicked-from-under-us>.

145 John Birmingham, 'The Year of Lethal Wonders' in Cunningham (n 130) 11, 15.

146 Ibid 16.

147 See Calla Wahlquist, '"This Lockdown Seems Different": Second Time Around, Melbourne Is on Edge', *The Guardian* (online, 9 July 2020) <www.theguardian.com/world/2020/jul/09/this-lockdown-seems-different-second-time-around-melbourne-is-on-edge>.

148 Madeleine Watts, *The Inland Sea* (ONE, 2020).

149 Ibid 215.

150 Adcock (n 134).

151 Watts (n 148) 225–7.

152 See, eg, Rob Harris, 'Australia to Join 100 Nations in Climate Resilience Pledge ahead of UN Summit', *The Sydney Morning Herald* (online, 25 January 2021) <www.smh.com.au/politics/federal/australia-to-join-100-nations-in-climate-resilience-pledge-ahead-of-un-summit-20210124-p56wg8.html>.

153 Natural Disasters Royal Commission Report (n 8) 29–30.

154 Lesley Head, 'Transformative Change Requires Resisting a New Normal' (2020) 10 *Nature Climate Change* 173, 174.

155 See Bradley Garrett, *Bunker: Building for the End Times* (Allen Lane, 2020).

156 Daniel Aldana Cohen, 'New York City as "Fortress of Solitude" after Hurricane Sandy: A Relational Sociology of Extreme Weather's Relationship to Climate Politics' (2020) *Environmental Politics*:1–21, 15 <https://doi.org/10.1080/09644016.2020.1816380>.

157 Ibid 8.

158 Ibid 13.

159 Ibid 15.

160 Beth Hill, 'Between Bushfire and Climate Change: Uncertainty, Silence and Anticipation Following the October 2013 Fires in the Blue Mountains, Australia' (PhD Thesis, The University of Sydney, 2017).

161 Ibid 136–7.

162 Ibid 158.

163 Watts (n 148) 121.

164 Ibid 52.

165 Anderson et al (n 143) 621.

166 Ibid 623.

167 See, eg, Freya Mathews (ed), *Ecology and Democracy* (Routledge, 1996).

168 Tim Flannery, *The Weather Makers: The History and Future Impact of Climate Change* (Text Publishing, 2005) 291.

169 Naomi Oreskes and Erik M Conway, *The Collapse of Western Civilization: A View from the Future* (Columbia University Press, 2014).

170 Philip Alston, *Climate Change and Poverty: Report of the Special Rapporteur on Extreme Poverty and Human Rights*, UN Doc A/HRC/41/39 (25 June 2019) 15.

171 Bonnie Honig, *Emergency Politics: Paradox, Law, Democracy* (Princeton University Press, 2009).

172 Robyn Eckersley, 'Geopolitan Democracy in the Anthropocene' (2017) 65(4) *Political Studies* 983, 996.

173 Luisa Neubauer, Greta Thunberg, Anuna de Wever van der Heyden and Adélaïde Charlier, 'Open Letter and Demands to EU and Other Leaders' (July 2020) <climateemergencyeu.org>.
174 Laura Devaney et al, 'Ireland's Citizens' Assembly on Climate Change: Lessons for Deliberative Public Engagement and Communication' (2020) 14(2) *Environmental Communication* 141, 141.
175 Ibid 142.
176 See Oscar Berglund and Daniel Schmidt, *Extinction Rebellion and Climate Change Activism: Breaking the Law to Change the World* (Palgrave Macmillan, 2020) 71.
177 Ibid 67–8, 70–1.
178 Danielle Celermajer and Dalia Nassar, 'COVID and the Era of Emergencies: What Type of Freedom Is at Stake?' (2020) 7(2) *Democratic Theory* 12, 21.
179 Berglund and Schmidt (n 176) 63.
180 Dana James and Trevor Mack, 'Towards an Ethics of Decolonizing Allyship in Climate Organizing: Reflections on Extinction Rebellion Vancouver' (2020) 11 *Journal of Human Rights and the Environment* 32, 52.
181 Mark O'Connell characterises Auschwitz thus, in Mark O'Connell, *Notes from an Apocalypse: A Personal Journey to the End of the World and Back* (Granta, 2020) 207.
182 Ibid 182.
183 Prithvi Varatharajan, 'Archives of Loss' (30 November 2020) *Sydney Review of Books* <https://sydneyreviewofbooks.com/review/living-with-the-anthropocene>.
184 Anderson et al (n 143) 622.
185 Quoted in Veronica Sullivan, '"Speculative Fiction Is a Powerful Political Tool": From War of the Worlds to Terra Nullius', *The Guardian* (online, 22 August 2017) <www.theguardian.com/books/australia-books-blog/2017/aug/22/speculative-fiction-is-a-powerful-political-tool-from-war-of-the-worlds-to-terra-nullius>.
186 Megan Davis and Nicole Watson, '"It's the Same Old Song": Draconian Counter-Terrorism Laws and the Déjà Vu of Indigenous Australians' (2006) 5(1) *Borderlands e-Journal*.
187 Victoria Grieves, 'A New Sovereign Republic: Living History in the Present' (2018) 60 *Griffith Review* 82, 83–4.
188 Ibid 84 (emphasis in original).
189 Melissa Lucashenko, 'Too Deadly: Coronavirus in Black Australia' in Cunningham (n 130) 135, 135–6.
190 *The Uluru Statement from the Heart* (2017) <https://ulurustatement.org/the-statement>.
191 Client Earth, 'Climate Threatened Torres Strait Islanders Bring Human Rights Claim against Australia' (Press Release, 12 May 2019) <www.clientearth.org/press/climate-threatened-torres-strait-islanders-bring-human-rights-claim-against-australia>.
192 *Mabo v Queensland (No 2)* [1991–92] 175 CLR 1, 60 (Brennan J).
193 Katharine Murphy, 'Australia Asks UN to Dismiss Torres Strait Islanders' Claim Climate Change Affects Their Human Rights', *The Guardian* (online, 14 August 2020) <www.theguardian.com/australia-news/2020/aug/14/australia-asks-un-to-dismiss-torres-strait-islanders-claim-climate-change-affects-their-human-rights>.
194 Ibid.

195 Victor Steffensen, *Fire Country: How Indigenous Fire Management Could Help Save Australia* (Hardie Grant Travel, 2020).
196 Bhiamie Williamson, Francis Markham and Jessica Weir, 'Aboriginal Peoples and the Response to the 2019–2020 Bushfires' (CAEPR Working Paper 134/2020, March 2020) 1.
197 Ibid 3.
198 Ibid 5.
199 Evidence to Royal Commission into National Natural Disaster Arrangements, Canberra, 18 June 2020, 800 (Bhiamie Eckford-Williamson).
200 Quoted in Chris Graham, 'Lost Country: Aboriginal Flags Have Begun Flying at Half Mast around Australia', *New Matilda* (online, 17 January 2020) <https://newmatilda.com/2020/01/17/for-country-lost-aboriginal-flags-have-begun-flying-at-half-mast-around-australia>.
201 Paola Balla, 'Tyirrum: The End of the World as We Knew It' (10 February 2020) *Sydney Review of Books* <https://sydneyreviewofbooks.com/essay/tyirrem-the-end-of-the-world-as-we-knew-it> (emphasis in original).
202 Quoted in Lorena Allam, 'Grave Fears Held for Hundreds of Important NSW South Coast Indigenous Sites', *The Guardian* (online, 16 January 2020) <www.theguardian.com/australia-news/2020/jan/15/grave-fears-held-for-hundreds-of-important-nsw-south-coast-indigenous-sites>.
203 Lorena Allam, 'For First Nations People the Bushfires Bring a Particular Grief, Burning What Makes Us Who We Are', *The Guardian* (online, 6 January 2020) <www.theguardian.com/commentisfree/2020/jan/06/for-first-nations-people-the-bushfires-bring-a-particular-grief-burning-what-makes-us-who-we-are>.
204 Williamson et al (n 196) 10.
205 Allam (n 203).
206 Raw law is a term devised by First Nations scholar Irene Watson, to encompass 'a natural system of obligations and benefits, flowing from an Aboriginal ontology': Irene Watson, *Aboriginal Peoples, Colonialism and International Law. Raw Law* (Routledge, 2015) 1.
207 Deborah Bird Rose, *Wild Dog Dreaming: Love and Extinction* (University of Virginia Press, 2011) 86.
208 Ibid 3.
209 Deborah Bird Rose, *Report from a Wild Country: Ethics for Decolonisation* (University of New South Wales Press, 2004) 65.
210 Mary Annaise Heglar, '2020: The Year of the Converging Crisis' (4 October 2020) *Rolling Stone* <www.rollingstone.com/politics/political-commentary/2020-crises-wildfires-pandemic-election-climate-crisis-1069907>.
211 Griffiths (n 130) 53.
212 Lorena Allam, '"National Emergency": Urgent Leadership Needed after Fifth Aboriginal Death in Custody since June', *The Guardian* (online, 20 September 2020) <www.theguardian.com/australia-news/2020/sep/20/national-emergency-urgent-leadership-needed-after-fifth-aboriginal-death-in-custody-since-june>.

3 Narratives of culpability

Nicole Rogers

In the previous chapter, I charted evolving discourses of emergency in a landmark year of climatic, social and economic disruption. Circling back to the theme of scalar framing in the Anthropocene, and the linked imperative of contemporaneously zooming in and out, I noted the temporal and cognitive barriers that constrain our understanding of chronic emergency and inhibit our response to it. In turning now to consider narratives of culpability and legality in the wake of Black Summer, scalar framing and the metaphor of zooming in and out provide, again, a useful framework to evaluate structural and conceptual shortcomings in existing legal responses to the megafires, and to the climate crisis generally.

My discussion proceeds as follows. I commence by acknowledging the 2020 inquiries that were established, at both State and Commonwealth levels, to investigate the megafires and provide recommendations to facilitate adaptation and preparation for future climate disasters. Importantly, causal factors were not a primary consideration for those undertaking these particular investigations, although the Natural Disasters Royal Commission recognised, in its final report, the unfolding panoply of related climate disasters that lie ahead. I then address culpability and associated legal narratives, broadening my focus, or zooming out, from the narratives of the individual and negligent State government department as culprit to the climate accountability of the federal government and corporate offenders.

I conclude this tale of law and blame by acknowledging fundamental barriers that prevent humanity, as a species, from accepting responsibility for the megafires, as part and symptom of the planetary disaster of the climate crisis. Here I investigate some of the boundaries to zooming out within our current systems of law and judging. At this juncture, the scalar limitations of law, and its inherent conceptual and imaginative failings, become evident.

DOI: 10.4324/b22677-3

Inquiries into the megafires

As previously flagged, the 2020 Royal Commission established by the federal government was given the official title of the Royal Commission into National Natural Disaster Arrangements. Virtual hearings began on 25 May 2020 and were streamed online in real time. This was the first Royal Commission into bushfires established by the federal government. The State governments have, however, instigated other Royal Commissions into previous catastrophic fires: namely, the Stretton Royal Commission following the Black Friday fires in Victoria in 1939, the 2009 Victorian Bushfires Royal Commission following the Black Saturday bushfires in Victoria and a 1961 Royal Commission into Western Australian bushfires. There have also been numerous inquiries into previous bushfires, undertaken at national, State and Territorial levels. Each of these Royal Commissions and inquiries has made recommendations, some of which have been adopted and implemented and some of which have not.

In addition to the Royal Commission, the worst affected States set up their own inquiries in the wake of the megafires. These were the Independent Inquiry into the 2019–2020 Victorian Fire Season, conducted by the Inspector-General for Emergency Management; the New South Wales Independent Bushfire Inquiry; an independent review undertaken by Queensland's Inspector-General Emergency Management into the State's bushfire preparedness, mitigation and overall firefighting response; and an independent review by the South Australian government, with prevention, preparation, response and recovery again being the dominant concerns. Furthermore, the Australian Senate established an inquiry into lessons to be learned in relation to the preparation and planning for, response to, and recovery efforts following the fires. By the end of 2020, these inquiries, with the exception of the Senate and Victorian inquiries, had concluded, and all had handed down reports[1] and recommendations. While the reports outlined various important strategies in relation to climate adaptation, none directly addressed culpability and, thus, the question of who, or what, could be held legally responsible for the megafires remained unanswered at governmental level.

Narratives of blame

The dearth of official statements on culpability can be contrasted with the prevalence of popular narratives in which blame has been assigned to a diverse group of culprits: the troubled young arsonist; the under-resourced government agencies that fail to 'manage', appropriately, public land such as national parks and State forests; the rapacious timber industry; the Carbon

Majors that drive the extraction and supply of fossil fuels; and State and federal governments in light of their failure to implement effective climate mitigation policies. In the following sections, I engage with various narratives of culpability, consider Australian lawsuits that adopt these narrative frameworks, and contemplate the relevance of the lawsuits in the context of global climate litigation.

#ArsonEmergency

In this particular narrative, the focus is upon the elusive figure of the arsonist as responsible culprit. There are precedents for the prosecution and conviction of arsonists in relation to other destructive Australian blazes; for instance, in 2012, a Victorian jury found Brendan Sokaluk guilty of 10 counts of arson causing death. Sokaluk deliberately lit the Churchill fire, one of the deadly Black Saturday fires in 2009.

In her 2018 non-fiction work *The Arsonist. A Mind on Fire*,[2] Chloe Hooper delves into Sokaluk's background, circumstances and motivations. He emerges as a pitiable character, seemingly incapable of understanding the consequences of his actions or even the ramifications of the guilty verdict due to an intellectual disability and autism.[3] As Hooper puts it, the arsonist 'likely inhabited an alternative reality'.[4]

Sokaluk was the only individual charged with offences arising from the Black Saturday fires. His defence team argued that he was 'easily scapegoated under the "pressure to somehow make someone responsible for a catastrophic occurrence"'.[5] In the aftermath of the fires, hate sites targeting Sokaluk sprang up on the internet; there was even a 'Brendan Sokaluk Must Burn In Hell' Facebook page.[6] Yet there were other responsible parties for the Black Saturday fires. The Victorian Bushfires Royal Commission found that five of the 11 major fires were caused by malfunctioning electricity infrastructure.[7]

The Royal Commission was less concerned with the role played by the Australian coal industry in global climate change, and the connection between climate change and the ferocity of the blaze.[8] One of the notable ironies in the prosecution of Sokaluk was the location of his hometown, and the blaze he started: in the mining region of Latrobe Valley with its large coal deposits and what was then an operational, mega-polluting power station.[9]

The arsonist is an archetypal figure, as Hooper points out, connected to mythical stories about fire thieves and tricksters.[10] As became apparent during Black Summer, he also provides a readily available scapegoat for those seeking to divert attention away from the connection between climate change and increasingly frequent and catastrophic bushfires.[11] In November 2019, in an editorial in the News Corp-owned *Australian* newspaper, a cartoonist was praised for 'cut[ting] through the nonsense and sanctimony' with his 'brattish little arsonist sitting on his mother's lap being told, "Don't blame yourself darling, that bushfire you lit was caused by climate change"'.[12] Two months later, at the height of the megafires, the putative contribution of arsonists to the crisis was still emphasised in the same publication; two journalists identified over 180 alleged arson cases since the beginning of 2019, and referred to the view of an expert that 50% of bushfires were lit by 'firebugs'.[13] This claim was later repeated in other News Corp-owned media outlets around the world.[14] Right-wing commentators seized upon the arsonist as the culpable party, thereby deflecting attention away from climate change as a key causal factor. The hashtag #ArsonEmergency was widely circulated on Twitter by bots and trolls.[15]

This explanation did not reflect the reality. In January 2020, the Victorian police rejected claims that the fires in East Gippsland and north-east Victoria were caused by arson.[16] Researchers have identified lightning as the causal factor behind 82% of Victoria's fires during Black Summer.[17] Similarly, in its final report, the New South Wales Bushfire Inquiry concluded that instances of suspected arson in the State made up only 'a very small proportion of the area burnt'.[18] Of the fires identified by the New South Wales Rural Fire Service as the most significant fires of the season, the vast majority were started by lightning strikes.[19]

In 2007, Cass Sunstein sought to explain the divergent reactions to terrorism and climate change. A number of factors came into play here, he believed, including the absence of a 'salient event' that represented climate risks in the way that the September 11 attacks highlighted the risks of terrorism, and the fact that the sources of climate change 'lack faces'.[20] He pointed out that public concern is intensified if blame can be directed at an adversary with 'a face and a narrative'.[21] At that time, most Americans believed that the risks associated with climate change would not manifest in the immediate future and would largely be faced by other nations.[22] If these factors also operate to explain Australian apathy and failure to address climate change, the megafires represent a significant turning point, constituting a salient event that clearly illustrates the magnitude of climate risks and Australia's own climate vulnerability. Locating 'identifiable perpetrator[s]' is another matter. Part of the attractiveness of the arsonist theory is that blame can be directed towards particular dysfunctional individuals.

Media misrepresentation also played a key role in the circulation of another misconceived fire narrative during Black Summer: the narrative of hazard reduction burning. Both narratives are of interest in the ways in which they redirect blame and responsibility. The focus on the arsonist as culprit disrupts the narrative of intergenerational blame apparent in the youth climate activist movement. The arsonist is invariably a troubled youth, usually male, and it is his deviant behaviour, rather than the inaction and heedless complacency of the older generation, that is responsible for disaster. The narrative of hazard reduction burning, in which responsibility for uncontrollable megafires lies with misguided ecologists, government bureaucrats and proponents of 'greens policy',[23] deflects attention away from the federal and State governments' recalcitrance on climate policy.

Fighting fire with fire

In the narrative of preventative burning, blame is assigned to those government agencies and employees who fail to undertake appropriate levels of hazard reduction burning on public land. In February 2020, it was reported that six farmers, who suffered property damage as a consequence of a fire that began in the adjacent Guy Fawkes National Park, were threatening to seek compensation from the Department of Planning, Industry and Environment through a class action; their aim was to force the Department to allow grazing and controlled burning in the park.[24] According to one of the farmers, the firestorm was exacerbated by the dangerous fuel load in the national park, because 'everyone is too scared to burn anything'.[25]

Forest and national park mismanagement through failure to burn is viewed by many as a plausible explanation for the extreme destructiveness of twenty-first century fires. During Black Summer, this position was adopted by Prime Minister Scott Morrison, who stated in Parliament that hazard reduction burning was at least as important as emission reductions as a response to worsening fire seasons.[26] Later in 2020, President Trump claimed that forest mismanagement was the reason for the catastrophic fire season in California, Oregon and Washington State,[27] a reiteration of similar statements made by the President on Twitter and in person after the devastating Camp Fire in California in 2018.[28]

Victims and survivors of the Black Summer megafires have also adopted this explanation; one stated that 'when that bush burnt it was littered with 40 years of growth and with the right conditions it was a roar like you've never heard, it was just unbelievable'.[29] Landowners subsequently resorted to preventative burning on their own properties in regions severely impacted by the megafires.[30] Fire thus becomes part of a manageable narrative, with environmentalists and bureaucrats as scapegoats, human ignorance or negligence as the explanation, and a remedy at hand: the 'firestick'. Fire historian Stephen Pyne, who has traced the contentious history of the 'firestick' in Australia, cautions that '[t]he only fire will be feral fire' without the strategic use of this implement.[31]

Not everyone shares these views. Novelist Richard Flanagan compared Morrison's comments to Winston Churchill announcing during the Blitz 'that rubble removal was more important than dealing with the Luftwaffe in fighting Hitler'.[32] During Black Summer, Shane Fitzsimmons, then New South Wales Rural Fire Service Commissioner, stated that preventative burning was no panacea.[33] Greg Mullins has highlighted the uncontrollable spread of fire in cleared areas many metres from 'bushfire ember attack', and pointed out that fire can gain more traction in its passage through light fuel areas.[34]

Importantly, from a scientific perspective, the narrative of hazard reduction burning is a furphy. Researchers have concluded, in a number of studies,[35] that hazard reduction burning achieves little in extreme fire weather conditions. Furthermore, fires deliberately lit in such conditions cannot always be controlled, and can join existing blazes or become destructive megafires themselves; for instance, during Black Summer, an attempted backburn at Mount Wilson by the New South Wales Rural Fire Service spread rapidly, burning for 53 days and destroying 63,700 hectares.[36]

A counterargument has been presented by a number of ecologists: namely, that logging practices rather than a failure to clear or burn exacerbate the destructiveness of wildfires. In 2020, a group of scientists found 'compelling evidence' that logging made Australian forests more fire-prone and 'contributed to increased fire severity and flammability'. They observed the repeated occurrence of fire in many areas of logged and regenerated forests.[37] This alternative narrative holds less sway. Environmentalists struggled to prevent logging in remaining unburnt areas in the wake of Black Summer. In the successful pursuit, in January 2020, of an injunction to halt logging in various Victorian forest coupes, the environmental group Wildlife of the Central Highlands argued that the operations further jeopardised the habitat of bushfire-affected threatened species;[38] it is noteworthy that the susceptibility of logged areas to future fires was not raised.

The appeal of the narrative relating to hazard reduction burning is enhanced by the conflation of Indigenous land management practices with controlled burning strategies. Some proponents attempt to bolster their case by reference to the historic practices of caring for Country as carried out by First Nations people. These practices are attracting increasing interest as the imperatives of climate adaptation become apparent. Victor Steffensen, a fire custodian who has been described as 'the face of cultural burning', argues that 'Indigenous knowledge of fire is the key to adapting to climate change' and that climate change represents 'an exciting time, an opportunity'.[39]

Traditional Indigenous practices of cultural burning do not, however, translate easily or readily to the Australian colonised landscape in what Stephen Pyne calls the Pyrocene:[40] a new age of fire. They are not designed for strategic asset protection, which experts believe is one of the most effective roles for hazard reduction burning in this landscape.[41] Nor can they be applied uniformly across a wide variety of different landscapes. Greg Mullins has observed that such practices are 'highly nuanced' and non-transferable, in the sense that '[w]hat works in savannah in northern Queensland won't necessarily work in subtropical rainforests in northern NSW or eucalypt forests in Victoria'.[42]

When the New South Wales Bushfire Inquiry released its final report, prominent media outlets presented a recommended increase in hazard reduction burning by landowners as one of its key findings.[43] The Commissioners acknowledged a widespread perception in the community that high fuel loads and lack of hazard reduction burning were a contributing factor to the ferocity of the megafires but did not, in fact, endorse this viewpoint. Instead, they emphasised that the dryness of the fuel was the dominant contributing factor, that hazard reduction burning did not necessarily affect the spread and impact of the fires, particularly in extreme fire conditions, and that more research into this aspect of fire management was required.[44] They flagged the likelihood that worse fire seasons would make hazard reduction burning increasingly less effective.[45] Greens politician Justin Field, speaking in the New South Wales Parliament, asserted that media misrepresentation of the inquiry's findings was the result of the politicisation of an independent process by 'unknown people'.[46]

Perhaps in order to avoid a similar level of media misrepresentation, the three Commissioners on the Natural Disasters Royal Commission used bold print in stating their conclusion about the limitations of hazard reduction burning: 'We heard many perspectives from public submissions that describe prescribed burning as, in effect, a panacea – a solution to bushfire risk. It is not'.[47]

Government as climate culprit

The framing of the arsonist as perpetrator, and the narrative of hazard reduction burning, gloss over the culpability of bigger, more formidable entities, including the State and federal governments, for their omissions and obfuscations in relation to climate mitigation, and consequential contributory role in the Black Summer megafires.

It is difficult to disentangle the numerous omissions and actions on the part of the federal government that, collectively, contributed to the catastrophe of Black Summer. One prominent concern was its failure to prepare adequately for the fire season, despite numerous scientific warnings, the predictions of the Bureau of Meteorology, and the concerted efforts of a group of former fire and emergency service chiefs and deputy chiefs, throughout 2019, to alert the government as to what lay ahead.

In mid-2019, the federal government had been advised by one of its statutory agencies, the Bureau of Meteorology, of climate and weather forecasts that accurately predicted the severity and conditions of the forthcoming fire season; this evidence was provided to the Natural Disasters Royal Commission on its first day of hearings.[48] The Bureau provided more than 100 briefings to federal, State and Territory governments between April and November.[49] Greg Mullins has publicly stated that he and fellow former fire and emergency chiefs from every State and Territory, calling themselves Emergency Leaders for Climate Action, were stymied on numerous occasions in their efforts to warn the government of the impending dangers.[50] Their April request for a meeting with the Prime Minister was referred to Angus Taylor, the Minister for Energy and Emissions, in July; the meeting, which included the Minister for Emergency Affairs but not the Prime Minister, did not take place until 4 December and, by then, the calamitous fire season was well underway.[51] In its interim report, the 2020 Senate inquiry concluded that the warnings of the Emergency Leaders for Climate Action should not have been ignored and that, ‘despite the numerous warnings’, the federal government ‘showed a clear lack of preparedness’ for the fire season.[52]

Even more problematically, the government disregarded its own 2018 National Disaster Risk Reduction Framework, which flagged the imminence of natural disasters ‘on unimagined scales, in unprecedented combinations and in unexpected locations’, and the need to prepare for these.[53] A recommended national implementation plan had not been prepared prior to Black Summer.

Failure to heed warnings is one aspect of culpability, but playing an active role in exacerbating the magnitude of the disaster is even more damning. The federal government’s obstinate refusal to address the severity of the looming fire season was compounded by its climate denialism and laggardness in the area of climate policy. No member of the government directly lit the fires. The government’s accountability lies in its steadfast refusal to curb the extraction and export of fossil fuels, its dubious climate accounting ploys, and its recalcitrance in setting mitigation goals and targets.

Admittedly, it is climate inaction on a global rather than domestic scale that has created the phenomenon of supercharged megafires, and ushered the world into Pyne’s Pyrocene. This argument was made at the height of the Black Summer fires by the Prime Minister, who acknowledged the ‘link’ between global climate change and ‘the dryness of conditions in many places’, but insisted that ‘no response by any one government anywhere in the world can be linked to any one fire event’.[54] In so doing, he adopted a version of the ‘drop in the ocean’ approach,[55] deployed by mining companies in anti-coalmine litigation in Australia; the argument has also surfaced in climate mitigation lawsuits elsewhere.[56]

The fossil fuel industry and some governments, including the Australian government, have repeatedly emphasised the absence of a direct chain of causation between climate disasters and emissions from particular projects, or from certain sparsely populated, albeit wealthy nations. In addition, they stress the global insignificance of such emissions. Yet, as the author of a strongly worded editorial in the prestigious journal *Nature* wrote in January 2020, '[c]hange will come when everyone acts in concert' and all nations, including Australia, 'have to play their part'.[57] Or, as eminent British naturalist David Attenborough has expressed it, 'what [Australians] say, what you do, really, really matters'.[58]

Australia's climate record is shaming. In a 2020 Climate Performance Index, released in December 2019, Australia was ranked as the worst performing country on national and international climate policy.[59] As the bushfires raged, the Prime Minister assured the nation that he had no intention of changing his existing climate policies, and any suggestion that he should do so was nothing more than political point-scoring.[60] As major nations adopted net zero emissions targets throughout 2020, he refused to follow suit.[61] By the end of 2020, his rhetoric had somewhat changed,[62] possibly in response to the November election of a United States President committed to tackling the existential threat of climate change. Nevertheless, Morrison's recalcitrance in relation to emissions targets cost him a speaking spot at a prominent United Nations Climate Ambition Summit in December.[63] Much more than rhetoric was required to improve Australia's poor performance in this area, as was revealed in a 2020 Climate Transparency Report in which the authors compared the climate performance of the G20 countries.[64]

Youth vs government

Climate litigants all around the world are seeking to hold their governments to account for their failure to mitigate. Human rights, constitutional, public trust, administrative law and torts arguments have been raised in various lawsuits, with some singular successes. In particular, the triumphant conclusion[65] in the Dutch Supreme Court to the proceedings brought by the Dutch Urgenda foundation against the Netherlands government, after earlier landmark rulings in two lower courts, has been inspirational for the climate movement. In light of these developments, at the conclusion of Black Summer, there was a considerable amount of speculation about possible lawsuits against the Commonwealth government, and their potential for success. An online petition, calling for a class action lawsuit against the Morrison government for its failure to mitigate, attracted more than 60,000 signatures.[66]

The notable achievement of the Urgenda case was the judicial recognition of the Dutch government's duty of care to its citizenry in relation to the regulation of emissions. During Black Summer, legal academic Kate Galloway and barrister George Newhouse wrote separate opinion pieces[67] in which they both concluded that actions in negligence against the Australian government had only a poor chance of success. Nevertheless, a common law duty of care was at the centre of one of the innovative climate lawsuits launched against the federal government later in 2020. In *Sharma v Minister for Environment*,[68] eight teenagers mounted a class action against the federal Minister for the Environment, alleging that she owed young people a common law duty not to cause them harm in the exercise of her decision-making power about a proposed extension of Whitehaven's Vickery coalmine. They sought an injunction in the Federal Court. Another lawsuit,[69] brought by a twenty-three-year-old law student, was focused upon the government's failure to disclose and protect its bondholders from financial risks created by climate change; Katta O'Donnell's case is discussed further later in this chapter. In yet another legal tactic, two teenagers sought revocation of the federal government's approval of the Adani coalmine, on the basis that then Environment Minister Greg Hunt failed to adequately address climate impacts and, in particular, the implications of the mine for the future of the Great Barrier Reef, when he issued the approval in 2015.[70]

These initiatives share commonalities with contemporaneous lawsuits in other parts of the world, but one particular characteristic bears emphasising: the youth of the litigants. Youth class actions against governments have been commenced in a number of jurisdictions; of these, the landmark *Juliana* case against the United States government has attracted the most publicity. The young litigants are arguing here that the government's failure to act on climate change constitutes a breach of its atmospheric public trust obligations, as well as an abridgement of their constitutional rights.

The case, commenced in 2015 and scheduled for trial in 2018, was derailed when the defendants, after a number of attempts to have the proceedings dismissed or stayed, succeeded in having an interlocutory appeal heard by the Ninth Circuit Court of Appeals. That Court issued its order in January 2020,[71] with the majority judges holding that the claims were non-justiciable and could not proceed to trial. The litigants unsuccessfully sought a review of this decision in 2020. A motion to amend their complaint and seek declaratory relief was filed in March 2021.

Other youth climate lawsuits on foot during 2020 included: a challenge on appeal to the Norwegian Supreme Court by a Norwegian youth organisation, in conjunction with Greenpeace Nordic Association, to the Norwegian government's grant of oil and gas licences in the Barents Sea;[72] a youth class action against the Canadian government, on appeal to the Federal Court of Appeal;[73] another youth climate class action against the Canadian government in the Superior Court of Québec, also on appeal;[74] a 2019 petition[75] to the United Nations Committee on the Rights of the Child by Greta Thunberg and 15 other youth climate activists, alleging breaches of the United Nations *Convention on the Rights of the Child*[76] by five signatory nations; a 2020 constitutional challenge to the adequacy of Germany's recent climate protection law;[77] and the first climate lawsuit in the European Court of Human Rights, filed by four Portuguese children and two young adults against 33 governments in September 2020.[78] These young people were impelled to bring the lawsuit following devastating forest fires in Portugal in 2017.[79] The Youth Verdict case in the Queensland Land Court, discussed in the next section, is another example: a case that highlights the role of the fossil fuel industry in exacerbating climate change and hence in abridging the rights of young people.

Although all of these lawsuits are important, the case before the European Court of Human Rights is particularly significant, given the status of the Court and the value of the case in setting a precedent. In November 2020, the Court announced its intention to expedite the proceedings in light of the urgency of the climate crisis.[80] The defendants' attempt to overturn this decision was unsuccessful.

Corporate offenders

A number of class actions were instigated after Black Summer. These included the Sharma youth lawsuit against the federal Minister for the Environment; a class action by bushfire survivors against the New South Wales Environment Protection Authority;[81] and the Youth Verdict lawsuit. Of these, only the last involved a corporate offender, and that corporation was not directly targeted, or framed as culpable in the lawsuit, which took the form of an objection to Waratah Coal's Galilee Coal project in the Queensland Land Court. The nature of the lawsuit, in which litigants sought to break new ground by invoking the very recently enacted Queensland *Human Rights Act 2019* in relation to decision-making in the Land Court, precluded this framing. The structural parameters of the legal proceedings have not, however, prevented the public dissemination of a narrative of plucky, desperate youngsters pitted against maverick billionaire and mining magnate Clive Palmer: the owner of Waratah Coal and the prominent figure behind the proposed coalmine.[82]

As one commentator has noted, courts respond well to narratives of environmental justice 'featuring sympathetic protagonists facing a villainous obstacle'.[83] One of the 'sympathetic protagonists' in the Youth Verdict case, Lily Kerley, has explained that the encroachment of fire on her family home during Black Summer 'made me realise that [climate change is] happening right now' and inspired her to take action.[84] The group, in conjunction with its co-litigant the Bimblebox Alliance, had an initial victory in September 2020 when President Kingham rejected Waratah Coal's application to dismiss their objection, holding that the Land Court was required under the 2019 Act to consider human rights in making its recommendations.[85] A number of hurdles remain to be overcome; these include, as Justine

Bell-James and Briana Collins have pointed out in relation to a hypothetical challenge of this kind, the breadth of the court's interpretation of the right to life, the court's willingness to engage with climate change arguments, and issues of causation.[86]

Other large fire events have spawned class actions against power companies. The 2009 Black Saturday fires led to two class actions in the Victorian Supreme Court, both of which settled with victims receiving a record amount of compensation.[87] After the Blue Mountains bushfire in 2013, which destroyed 196 houses and damaged many others, those directly affected launched a class action against Endeavour Energy in the New South Wales Supreme Court. They argued that the power company should have been aware of the dangers posed by a rotten tree, which fell upon a power line at Springwood.[88] That case settled in 2016. Similarly, in March 2021, a class action lawsuit against the South Australian energy distributor was mounted in the South Australian Supreme Court; the litigants are alleging that its inadequate fault protection settings caused the Cudlee Creek bushfire during Black Summer.[89]

Liability of power companies is a common theme in other jurisdictions. Between 2014 and 2017, poorly maintained infrastructure owned and operated by Pacific Gas and Electric, California's largest electricity supplier, caused at least 1500 fires.[90] The company was responsible for five of the 10 most destructive fires in California between 2015 and 2019.[91] These included the notorious Camp Fire that destroyed the town of Paradise, killed 85 people, and was the most expensive natural disaster of 2018.[92] The company subsequently declared bankruptcy, to avoid an estimated liability of more than $30 billion.[93] In June 2020, its chief executive pleaded guilty to 84 counts of involuntary manslaughter, in relation to the deaths caused by the Camp Fire, and one count of illegally setting a fire.[94]

Here we see, as Stephen Pyne has put it, a direct point of intersection between the burning of fossil fuels or 'lithic landscapes', and the burning of living landscapes.[95] Yet a further, even more contentious connection exists between these two 'realms of fire'.[96] The wildfires of this decade are supercharged by climate change and the ensuing liability issues are far more complex, as I discuss in the next section.

Ironically, the same judge who was prepared to hold Pacific Gas and Electric responsible for the Camp Fire, despite the role of other contributing factors including climate change, was not prepared to hold the Carbon Majors responsible for major infrastructure costs associated with climate change impacts. Judge Alsup was overseeing the corporation's probation at the time of the Camp Fire, after its breaches of federal pipeline safety regulations.[97] He publicly castigated the company for its failure to take responsibility for the fires,[98] stating that it was 'unthinkable that a public utility would be out there causing that kind of damage'.[99] Yet when it came to the Carbon Majors, their indisputable contribution to the climate crisis, and the present and future impacts of that crisis, he was far more reticent.

The climate culpability of the Carbon Majors[100]

In 2017, various public authorities across the United States began a concerted legal campaign to hold the Carbon Majors to account for the economic burden of climate adaptation. Lawsuits have been instigated by cities, municipalities and States against the most prominent Carbon Majors, alleging, inter alia, public nuisance, private nuisance, trespass and violations of State consumer fraud statutes. Most of these have been stalled by jurisdictional wrangling, as the well-resourced defendants have sought, thus far unsuccessfully, to have them moved from State courts to the federal courts.

Establishing a direct chain of causation between the poorly maintained infrastructure of power companies and the ignition of specific fires is relatively straightforward. It is more challenging to demonstrate, in a courtroom setting, the causal links between the quantifiable contribution of one or more of the Carbon Majors to global greenhouse gas emissions, and climate impacts such as flooding, sea level rise or, indeed, megafires. Here the arguments of litigants are boosted by the work of geographer Richard Heede and the Climate Accountability Institute in attribution science. In 2013, Heede provided quantitative evidence of the overwhelming contribution of 90 'Carbon Major' entities to the rise in global greenhouse gas emissions; they have contributed nearly two thirds of industrial greenhouse gas emissions.[101] In 2019, new data demonstrated that the top 20 fossil fuel companies have collectively produced 35% of all fossil fuel emissions worldwide since 1965, largely from the combustion of their products.[102]

A promising international development in the area of climate attribution was a 2017 German appellate ruling, which permitted the case brought by Peruvian citizen Saúl Luciano Lliuya against Germany's largest electricity corporation to proceed into its evidentiary phase.[103] Lliuya is seeking 0.47% of the cost of flood mitigation works to protect his house from a melting glacier, on the basis that the corporation contributes 0.47% of annual global greenhouse gas emissions. Also significant in this context was the finding of the Philippino Human Rights Commission, announced in December 2019, that 47 Carbon Majors are legally and morally liable for human rights violations. The inquiry was instigated in 2015 after super typhoon Haiyan wreaked havoc throughout the Philippines.

There has yet to be a successful outcome in any of the American lawsuits. In the case brought by the City of Oakland and San Francisco, Judge Alsup held that the claims were non-justiciable. He also, in stark contrast to his condemnation of Pacific Gas and Electricity, hesitated to admonish fossil fuel companies for delivering products used by consumers worldwide, stating that it might not be fair to 'ignore our own responsibility in the use of fossil fuels and place the blame for global warming on those who supplied what we demanded'.[104]

In Australia, attribution lawsuits have not yet been mounted against the Carbon Majors, although in December 2018 the Climate Minister in the Australian Capital Territory said that his government was exploring this option.[105] One Australian company constitutes an obvious target: BHP Billiton, which appears in the Climate Accountability Institute's top 20 list of Carbon Majors in terms of its contribution to the climate crisis between 1965 and 2017.[106] Yet BHP is not the only Carbon Major in Australia. Ten Australian companies, by producing and selling fossil fuels, are responsible for more emissions than Canada.[107]

Australian climate litigants are, instead, utilising provisions outlining directors' duties in corporations law, and analogous provisions elsewhere. In November 2020, Mark McVeigh's action against his superannuation fund, on the basis of its failure to disclose climate change business risks in accordance with its duties under the *Corporations Act 2001* (Cth), settled; the fund conceded that it needed to address these risks proactively. This outcome was heralded as groundbreaking.[108] Katta O'Donnell's lawsuit against the Australian government, commenced in July 2020, draws upon a comparable provision in the *Public Governance, Performance and Accountability Act 2013* (Cth) in relation to its trade in government bonds; section 25 requires Commonwealth officials to act with the standard of care and diligence of a reasonable person in their position. O'Donnell's concerns about climate change were reportedly heightened by the 2009 Black Saturday fires and the Black Summer megafires.[109] Both cases emphasise the nature of climate change as financial risk; there are legal obligations on 'market actors' to both 'disclose and address' this risk.[110]

Another legal strategy pertaining to the corporate obligations of market actors was a complaint process against the ANZ bank, instigated by Friends of the Earth in conjunction with three megafire survivors in January 2020. The complainants alleged that the ANZ's funding of fossil fuel projects and failure to disclose associated climate impacts put it in breach of the Organisation for Economic Co-operation and Development (OECD) guidelines for corporate conduct. An initial assessment by the Australian National Contact Point for the OECD guidelines was released in November 2020.[111] In October, the ANZ had announced that its funding of thermal coal will cease by 2030.

Civil lawsuits and strategies can be contrasted with punitive proceedings: the prosecution and sentencing of climate criminals. Climate criminality became an increasingly contentious topic of discussion throughout 2020. In this context, the individuals who control and direct the Carbon Majors, and are thereby complicit in the carbon emitting activities of these corporations, as well as political leaders who have impeded global efforts to reduce emissions, are potential defendants.

Climate criminality

Two criminologists have noted that '[t]he literature on climate change is replete with the language of crime and criminality'.[112] The concept of environmental crime or ecocide has been gaining some traction both in popular debate and in the legal arena, as I discuss shortly. An even more ambitious criminal category was proposed in response to the devastation of Black Summer.

In January 2020, philosopher Danielle Celermajer, whose property in the Southern Highlands of New South Wales was directly impacted by the blazes, wrote a searing piece for the Australian Broadcasting Corporation.[113] She extrapolated from Raphael Lemkin's search for an appropriate term to encompass the crimes of the Holocaust, an endeavour that culminated in the creation of the offence of genocide in international human rights law, and suggested that a similarly novel offence should be recognised and prosecuted in the wake of the destruction of the megafires: that of omnicide, or the killing of everything.

Supporters of this idea include novelist Richard Flanagan, who singled out Prime Minister Morrison as the pre-eminent guilty party: 'faced with the historic tragedy of his country's destruction, [Morrison] dissembled, enabled, subsidized and oversaw omnicide, until all was ash and even the future was no more'.[114] Prominent theorist Noam Chomsky agreed; he identified Morrison's government, together with the United States Trump administration and Bolsonaro's government in Brazil, as the three most destructive, climate criminals on Earth, guilty of the 'worst crimes in Earth's history'.[115] Another writer described the perpetrators of omnicide as 'ecopaths', who 'kill the conditions for life itself' and 'roam free in the lag between the triggers they pull today and the corpses that pile up in the future'.[116]

Formulating a new criminal concept is, arguably, less challenging than creating or adapting legal systems within which prosecutions can occur. The crime of ecocide has not yet been incorporated within the Rome Statute as a fifth crime against peace, to be tried in the International Criminal Court, notwithstanding years of campaigning by activists such as the late Polly Higgins,[117] and French President Emmanuel Macron's endorsement of the term. In 2019, the President described the fires that were burning in the Amazon forest as 'an international crisis' and the consequence of 'a real ecocide'.[118] In June 2020, a French citizens' assembly convened by the President, the Convention Citoyenne pour le Climat, voted to make ecocide a crime; President Macron subsequently indicated that he will investigate ways to incorporate ecocide into French law and lobby for its recognition as a crime in international law.[119] At the end of 2020, the French government outlined its proposed ecocide law.[120] At the same time, a panel of leading lawyers was independently convened to create a legal definition of ecocide as an international crime.[121]

Identifying defendants could also prove to be unexpectedly complicated. This problem, in a more manageable form, was faced by the Allied forces when orchestrating the Nuremburg Trials; it was decided to prosecute only the Nazi ringleaders. There were, however, countless others implicated in the Holocaust.

Civil actions against the Carbon Majors, such as those discussed in the previous section, or criminal proceedings against the chief executive officers and directors of those corporations, are aligned with what two international relations scholars have identified as extractivist discourse: '[r]ather than presenting the Anthropocene as the aggregated effect of an undifferentiated humanity, the extractivist world directs blame and liability' at the global capitalist system and its key players.[122] Criminal proceedings against certain political leaders in the Global North also form part of this discourse.

Zooming out beyond the key tenets of extractivist discourse allows for the possibility of prosecuting, or punishing, non-individuated multitudes. Although some individuals, and certain national and social groupings, are more culpable than others, it is the human species that constitutes the geological force responsible for the ecological and climate crisis. Can 'the Leviathon of humanity en masse',[123] to adopt Timothy Clark's phrase, be tried for omnicide?

Putting humanity on trial

The planetary scale of the climate crisis, and the miniscule but indisputable contribution that, to varying degrees, each human being makes, is an unavoidable part of any discussion around culpability. Timothy Morton has reflected that every time he turns on his car engine, an action devoid of 'statistical meaning' or malicious intent, he is implicated in the hyperobject of climate change.[124] Hyperobjects, he writes, 'make hypocrites of us all'; 'we are always in the wrong'.[125] He draws an analogy with noir fiction: the 'human hyperobject',[126] but in particular the citizens of the Global North, share the roles of detective and criminal.[127] Even the narrator, as in 'a strong version of noir', is implicated in the story as the 'tragic criminal'.[128] Furthermore, all of humanity is destined to fall victim to climate change, albeit at different times and in varying degrees. There is, as Beth Hill puts it, a 'charged connection between vulnerability and responsibility'.[129]

Danielle Celermajer argues that 'responsibility for omnicide is various and layered'. Rapacious consumers, the deliberately ill-informed and those who 'prioritise short-term interests over the sustainability of the natural world' share this responsibility with more egregious offenders, including certain politicians, corporate figures, media owners, financial institutions and investors. Climate change is attributable to a species, rather than a matter of individual responsibility;[130] how, then, can culpability be assigned? The paradigm shift required in envisaging a process that would put humanity as a species on trial speaks to the difficulties with judging on a planetary scale; thought experiments in planetary justice[131] and Earth system law[132] are still nascent. As Morton puts it, '[h]umanistic tools for thought at Earth magnitude are lacking and often because we have deliberately resisted fashioning them'.[133]

The scalar limitations of law are evident in most climate lawsuits. The 'rights turn' in contemporary climate litigation, as identified by Jacqueline Peel and Hari Osofsky,[134] is, for instance, a prime example of a reductionist framing. The rights turn is almost entirely about *human* rights,[135] and at the heart of this framing is a paradox: the exercise of certain rights, including communal development rights, individual rights of movement and both individual and corporate property rights exacerbate the climate crisis but, conversely, the climate emergency jeopardises all these rights and many others. Despite the paradoxical and reductionist quality of rights-based climate lawsuits, their utility to the climate movement is evident. The language of rights is a language that the legal system recognises and understands. On the other hand, as Timothy Clark has pointed out, rights-based arguments intended to distribute more broadly the trappings of Western prosperity resemble, when viewed at a different scale, 'an insane plan to destroy the biosphere'.[136]

To reflect upon the culpability of humanity as a species is a necessary part of understanding and responding to the climate crisis. Nevertheless, the fundamental requirement of intra-species justice demands that we zoom in as well. Zooming in enables us to identify major corporate and political culprits, whose climate crimes include obfuscation as well as enabling, and carrying out, the large-scale production of fossil fuels. Existing legal systems are equipped to evaluate the legal accountability of such parties for specific and future climate impacts. They are not well placed to deliberate on questions of interspecies or planetary justice.

Conclusion

This discussion of narratives of culpability demonstrates the difficulties in assigning blame and allocating legal responsibility for devastating climate disasters such as the megafires, and for the scalar phenomenon, or hyperobject, of climate change itself. Nevertheless, survivors and observers of climate disasters are impelled to seek out justice, of both corrective and punitive dimensions.

The instigation and pursuit of multiple lawsuits in the wake of the megafires indicates that fluctuations in discourses of emergency throughout 2020, as described in the previous chapter, had little impact on climate narratives of culpability and lawfulness. Litigants, and in particular youth litigants, were not dissuaded by the pandemic and its associated restrictions from seeking climate remedies in courtrooms.

In the next chapter, I consider the evolution of climate narratives of activism in 2020. Here we find a dramatic fallout from the pandemic and its restrictions, and an increased awareness of the interconnections between social justice movements and the climate emergency.

Notes

1 Inspector-General for Emergency Management, *Independent Inquiry into the 2019–20 Victorian Fire Season – Phase 1 Report* (31 July 2020); *Final Report of the NSW Bushfire Inquiry* (31 July 2020) ('NSW Inquiry Final Report'); Inspector-General Emergency Management, *Queensland Bushfires Review Report 2: 2019–20* (10 February 2020); South Australian Independent Bushfire Review Team, *Independent Review into South Australia's 2019–20 Bushfire Season* (June 2020); The Senate, Finance and Public Administration References Committee, *Lessons to Be Learned in Relation to the Australian Bushfire Season 2019–20* (Interim Report, 2020) ('Senate Interim Report').
2 Chloe Hooper, *The Arsonist: A Mind on Fire* (Hamish Hamilton, 2018).
3 Ibid 163.
4 Ibid 166.
5 Ibid 162.
6 Ibid 114.
7 *2009 Victorian Bushfires Royal Commission* (Final Report, July 2010) vol 2, 148.
8 Climate change did not appear in the terms of reference and was barely mentioned in the final report. Paddy Manning notes that, for this reason, the Commission was called the 'Royal Omission': Paddy Manning, *Body Count: How Climate Change Is Killing Us* (Simon and Schuster, 2020) 51.
9 Hooper (n 2) 138–40.
10 Ibid 233.
11 Greenpeace Australia Pacific, *Dirty Power, Burnt Country: How the Fossil Fuel Industry, News Corp, and the Federal Government Hijacked the Black Summer Bushfires to Prevent Action on Climate Change* (Report, May 2020) 38.
12 Chris Kenny, 'Climate Alarmists are Brazen Opportunists Preying on Misery', *The Australian* (online, 15 November 2019) <www.theaustralian.com.au/inquirer/climate-alarmists-are-brazen-opportunists-preying-on-misery/news-story/00d6187186abc4b74e46f7d2b7903053>.
13 David Ross and Imogen Reid, 'Bushfires: Firebugs Fuelling Crisis as National Arson Toll Hits 183', *The Australian* (online, 15 January 2020) <www.theaustralian.com.au/nation/bushfires-firebugs-fuelling-crisis-asarson-arresttollhits183/news-story/52536dc9ca9bb87b7c76d36ed1acf53f>.

14 'News Corp's Fire Fight', *ABC Media Watch* (online, 3 February 2020) <www.abc.net.au/mediawatch/episodes/news-corp-fire/11925590>. See, also, a discussion of the role of News Corp in disseminating misinformation about arson in Greenpeace Australia Pacific's *Dirty Power, Burnt Country* report: Greenpeace Australia Pacific (n 11) 33–8.

15 Timothy Graham and Tobias R Keller, 'Bushfires, Bots and Arson Claims: Australia Flung in the Global Disinformation Spotlight', *The Conversation* (online, 10 January 2020) <https://theconversation.com/bushfires-bots-and-arson-claims-australia-flung-in-the-global-disinformation-spotlight-129556>.

16 Paul Sakkal, 'Victoria Police Rejects Social Media Campaign Claiming Arson Caused Fires', *The Age* (online, 9 January 2020) <www.theage.com.au/national/victoria/victoria-police-rejects-social-media-campaign-claiming-arson-caused-fires-20200108-p53pwj.html>.

17 Diane Cook, 'Open Data Shows Lightning, Not Arson, Was the Likely Cause of Most Victorian Bushfires Last Summer', *The Conversation* (online, 18 December 2020) <https://theconversation.com/open-data-shows-lightning-not-arson-was-the-likely-cause-of-most-victorian-bushfires-last-summer-151912>.

18 NSW Inquiry Final Report (n 1) 29.

19 Ibid 24.

20 Cass R Sunstein, 'On the Divergent Reactions to Terrorism and Climate Change' (2007) 107 *Columbia Law Review* 503, 507.

21 Ibid 543.

22 Ibid 507.

23 Graham Readfearn, 'Factcheck: Is There Really a Green Conspiracy to Stop Bushfire Hazard Reduction?', *The Guardian* (online, 12 November 2019) <www.theguardian.com/australia-news/2019/nov/12/is-there-really-a-green-conspiracy-to-stop-bushfire-hazard-reduction>.

24 Quoted in Andrew Messenger, 'Bushfire Lawsuit: Armidale Farmers Say Burnoffs Could Have Stopped Bees Nest Blaze, Threaten to Sue', *Glen Innes Examiner* (online, 4 February 2020) <www.gleninnesexaminer.com.au/story/6613307/bushfire-lawsuit-farmers-threaten-to-sue-national-parks-to-force-more-burnoffs>.

25 Alexandra Smith, '"We Saw This Coming for Years": Farmers Take Legal Action after Fires', *The Sydney Morning Herald* (online, 6 February 2020) <www.smh.com.au/politics/nsw/we-saw-this-coming-for-years-farmers-take-legal-action-after-fires-20200206-p53ygl.html>.

26 Adam Morton, 'Hazard Reduction Burning Had Little to No Effect in Slowing Extreme Bushfires', *The Guardian* (online, 6 February 2020) <www.theguardian.com/environment/2020/feb/06/hazard-reduction-burning-had-little-to-no-effect-in-slowing-this-summers-bushfires>.

27 Farrah Tomazin, 'Trump Breaks Silence on Devastating Wildfires, Blaming Them on Bad Forest Management', *The Sydney Morning Herald* (online, 13 September 2020) <www.smh.com.au/world/north-america/trump-breaks-silence-on-devastating-wildfires-blames-them-on-bad-forest-management-20200913-p55v64.html>.

28 Alistair Gee and Dani Anguiano, *Fire in Paradise: An American Tragedy* (WW Norton, 2020) 172, 174.

29 Quoted in Michael McGowan, '"You Can See It in Their Eyes": Long after the Bushfires the Pain Lingers in Cobargo', *The Guardian* (online, 25 July 2020) <www.theguardian.com/australia-news/2020/jul/25/you-can-see-it-in-their-eyes-long-after-the-bushfires-the-pain-lingers-in-cobargo>.

30 Damien Cave, 'Australia's Witnesses to Fire's Fury Are Desperate to Avoid a Sequel', *The New York Times* (online, 14 September 2020) <www.nytimes.com/2020/09/14/world/australia/bush-fires-preventive-burns.html>.

31 Stephen Pyne, *The Still-Burning Bush* (Scribe, rev ed, 2020) 144.

32 Richard Flanagan, 'How Does a Nation Adapt to Its Own Murder?', *The New York Times* (online, 25 January 2020) <www.nytimes.com/2020/01/25/opinion/sunday/australia-fires-climate-change.html>.

33 Sally Rawsthorne, 'Hazard Reduction Burns Are "Not the Panacea": RFS Boss', *The Sydney Morning Herald* (online, 8 January 2020) <www.smh.com.au/national/hazard-reduction-burns-are-not-the-panacea-rfs-boss-20200108-p53poq.html>.

34 Senate Interim Report (n 1) 58–9.

35 See, eg, Owen F Price et al, 'Biogeographical Variation in the Potential Effectiveness of Prescribed Fire in South-Eastern Australia' (2015) 42 *Journal of Biogeography* 2234; Kevin G Tolhurst and Greg McCarthy, 'Effect of Prescribed Burning on Wildfire Severity: A Landscape-Scale Case Study from the 2003 Fires in Victoria' (2016) 79 *Australian Forestry* 1. See also Trent Penman, Kate Parkins and Sarah McColl-Gausden, 'A Surprising Answer to a Hot Question: Controlled Burns Often Fail to Slow a Bushfire', *The Conversation* (online, 15 November 2019) <https://theconversation.com/a-surprising-answer-to-a-hot-question-controlled-burns-often-fail-to-slow-a-bushfire-127022>.

36 Harriet Alexander, 'The Hidden Bushfire: Inside the Blue Mountains Backburn', *The Sydney Morning Herald* (online, 19 November 2020) <www.smh.com.au/national/nsw/the-hidden-bushfire-inside-the-blue-mountains-backburn-20201110-p56daa.html>.

37 David B Lindenmayer et al, 'Recent Australian Wildfires Made Worse by Logging and Associated Forest Management' (2020) 4 *Nature, Ecology and Evolution* 898, 899.

38 *Wildlife of the Central Highlands Inc v VicForests* [2020] VSC 10.

39 'Fighting Fire with Fire/Victor Steffensen', *ABC Australian Story* (13 April 2020) <www.abc.net.au/austory/fighting-fire-with-fire/12134242>.

40 Pyne (n 31) 5; Stephen Pyne, 'The Fire Age' (5 May 2015) *Aeon* <https://aeon.co/essays/how-humans-made-fire-and-fire-made-us-human>.

41 See, eg, a 2020 CSIRO report in which the authors state that: 'Hazard reduction by individuals and communities in the immediate vicinity of homes and buildings can significantly reduce house and life loss'; CSIRO, *Climate and Disaster Resilience* (Report, 30 June 2020) 30.

42 Greg Callahan, '"Of One Thing We Can Be Certain, The Fires Will Return": Greg Mullins' Global Warning', *The Sydney Morning Herald* (online, 18 September 2020) <www.smh.com.au/environment/climate-change/of-one-thing-we-can-be-certain-the-fires-will-return-greg-mullins-global-warning-20200820-p55nmm.html>.

43 See, eg, Alexandra Smith and Peter Hannam, 'Landowners in Fire-Prone Areas to Be Required to Do Hazard Reduction Burns', *The Sydney Morning Herald* (online, 24 August 2020) <www.smh.com.au/national/nsw/landowners-in-fire-prone-areas-to-be-required-to-do-hazard-reduction-burns-20200824-p55or9.html>; Yoni Bashan, 'Black Summer Bushfire Inquiry: Clear Land, Cut Bushfire Risk', *The Australian* (online, 8 August 2020) <www.theaustralian.com.au/nation/politics/black-summer-bushfire-inquiry-clear-land-cut-bushfire-risk/news-story/d170e7af3f86c1070f012ead4bd9fd6e>.

44 NSW Inquiry Final Report (n 1) 47, 156.
45 Ibid 164.
46 Hansard, NSW Legislative Council, 26 August 2020, 31.
47 *Royal Commission into National Natural Disaster Arrangements* (Report, 28 October 2020) 375.
48 Calla Wahlquist, 'Australia's Severe Bushfire Season Was Predicted and Will Be Repeated, Inquiry Told', *The Guardian* (online, 25 May 2020) <www.theguardian.com/australia-news/2020/may/25/australias-severe-bushfire-season-was-predicted-and-will-be-repeated-inquiry-told>.
49 Senate Interim Report (n 1) 50.
50 Anne Davies, 'Australian Bushfires: How the Morrison Government Failed to Heed Warnings of Catastrophe', *The Guardian* (online, 3 June 2020) <www.theguardian.com/australia-news/2020/jun/03/australian-bushfires-fois-shed-new-light-on-why-morrison-government-was-ill-prepared>.
51 Evidence to Senate Finance and Public Administration References Committee, Parliament of Australia, Canberra, 27 May 2020, 5 (Greg Mullins).
52 Senate Interim Report (n 1) 65.
53 James Fernyhough, 'Government Buried Climate Risk Action Plan', *The Australian Financial Review* (online, 11 January 2020) <www.afr.com/politics/federal/government-buried-climate-risk-action-plan-20200110-p53qeg>.
54 Quoted in Stephanie Convery, 'Morrison's Government on the Bushfires: From Attacking Climate "Lunatics" to Calling in the Troops', *The Guardian* (online, 4 January 2020) <www.theguardian.com/australia-news/2020/jan/04/morrisons-government-on-the-bushfires-from-attacking-climate-lunatics-to-calling-in-the-troops>.
55 See Jacqueline Peel, 'Issues in Climate Change Litigation' (2011) 5(1) *Carbon and Climate Law Review* 15, 16–7.
56 For example, the Dutch government unsuccessfully raised this argument in *Urgenda v Netherlands*: see *Urgenda v Netherlands* (Hague District Court, ECLI:NL:RBDHA:2015:7196, 24 June 2015), *Netherlands v Urgenda* (The Hague Court of Appeal, ECLI:NL:GHDHA:2018:2610, 9 October 2018), and *Netherlands v Urgenda* (Supreme Court of the Netherlands, ECLI:NL:HR:2019:2007, 20 December 2019).
57 Editorial, 'Australia: Show the World What Climate Action Looks Like' (2020) 577 *Nature* 449.
58 Quoted in James Hennessy, 'Sir David Attenborough Has Slammed Australia's Belligerence on Coal and Climate Change, Saying the Country Doesn't "Give a Damn" about the Rest of the World', *Business Insider Australia* (online, 24 September 2019) <www.businessinsider.com.au/sir-david-attenborough-australia-climate-2019-9>.
59 Jan Burck et al, *Climate Change Performance Index: Results 2020* (Report, Germanwatch, NewClimate Institute and Climate Action Network International, 2019) 17 <https://newclimate.org/wp-content/uploads/2019/12/CCPI-2020-Results_Web_Version.pdf>.
60 Paul Karp, 'Scott Morrison Returns from Holiday and Signals No Change to Climate Policy Despite Bushfires Crisis', *The Guardian* (online, 22 December 2019) <www.theguardian.com/australia-news/2019/dec/22/scott-morrison-returns-from-holiday-and-signals-no-change-to-climate-policy-despite-bushfires-crisis>.
61 Katharine Murphy, 'Scott Morrison Refuses to Commit to Net Zero Emissions Target by 2050', *The Guardian* (online, 20 September 2020) <www.theguardian.

com/australia-news/2020/sep/20/scott-morrison-refuses-to-commit-to-net-zero-emissions-target-by-2050>.

62 Katharine Murphy and Adam Morton, 'Scott Morrison's Climate Language Has Shifted: But Actions Speak Louder Than Words', *The Guardian* (online, 29 November 2020) <www.theguardian.com/environment/2020/nov/29/scott-morrisons-climate-language-has-shifted-but-actions-speak-louder-than-words>.

63 Bevan Shields, 'UN Defends Excluding Morrison from Climate Summit, Canberra Livid with Johnson over Snub', *The Sydney Morning Herald* (online, 11 December 2020) <www.smh.com.au/world/europe/un-defends-excluding-morrison-from-climate-summit-canberra-livid-with-johnson-over-snub-20201211-p56mk7.html>

64 Catrina Godinho et al, *Climate Transparency Report: Comparing G20 Climate Action and Responses to the Covid-19 Crisis* (Report, 2020) <www.climate-transparency.org/g20-climate-performance/the-climate-transparency-report-2020>.

65 *Urgenda v Netherlands* (Supreme Court of the Netherlands, ECLI:NL:HR:2019:2007, 20 December 2019).

66 Dana Drugmand, 'Indonesian Flood Victims Launch Suit vs. Government', *Drilled News* (Blog Post, 21 January 2020) <www.drillednews.com/post/indonesian-flood-victims-launch-suit-vs-government>.

67 Kate Galloway, 'Analysis: Holding Government to Account', *Environmental Defenders Office* (Blog Post, 24 January 2020) <www.edo.org.au/2020/01/24/holding-govt-to-account>; George Newhouse, 'I've Won Cases against the Government Before: Here's Why I Doubt a Climate Change Class Action Would Succeed', *The Conversation* (online, 13 January 2020) <https://theconversation.com/ive-won-cases-against-the-government-before-heres-why-i-doubt-a-climate-change-class-action-would-succeed-129707>.

68 *Sharma v Minister for the Environment* (Federal Court of Australia).

69 *O'Donnell v Commonwealth* (Federal Court of Australia).

70 Stephen Long, 'Queensland Teenagers Lodge Legal Action against Adani Coal Mine to Save Great Barrier Reef', *ABC News* (online, 22 October 2020) <www.envirojustice.org.au/qld-teenagers-present-critical-new-evidence-to-revoke-approval-of-adani-coal-mine>.

71 *Juliana v United States* 947 F3d 1159 (9th Cir 2020).

72 In April 2020, the litigants were successful in having leave to appeal to the Norwegian Supreme Court granted, following adverse findings in the Oslo District Court (*Greenpeace Nordic Association v Ministry of Petroleum and Energy* (Oslo District Court, 16–166674TVI-OTIR/06, 4 January 2018) and Bogarting Court of Appeal (*Greenpeace Nordic Association v Ministry of Petroleum and Energy* (Bogarting Court of Appeal, 18–060499ASD-BORG/03).

73 *La Rose v the Queen* (Federal Court of Appeal); the plaintiffs are appealing the decision of the Federal Court in *La Rose v the Queen* 2020 FC 1008 to strike their Statement of Claim on the basis that the claims are non-justiceable.

74 *ENvironnement JEUnesse v Attorney General of Canada* (Superior Court of Québec).

75 *Sacchi v Argentina*, Petition submitted under Article 5 of the Third Optional Protocol to the United Nations *Convention on the Rights of the Child*, 23 September 2019.

76 *Convention on the Rights of the Child*, opened for signature 20 November 1989, 1577 UNTS 3 (entered into force 2 September 1990).

77 *Neubauer v Germany* (Federal Constitutional Court).

78 *Youth for Climate Justice v Austria* (European Court of Human Rights).
79 Chloé Farand, 'Six Portuguese Youth File "Unprecedented" Climate Lawsuit against 33 Countries', *Climate Change News* (online, 3 September 2020) <www.climatechangenews.com/2020/09/03/six-portuguese-youth-file-unprecedented-climate-lawsuit-33-countries>.
80 Jonathan Watts, 'European States Ordered to Respond to Youth Activists' Climate Lawsuit', *The Guardian* (online, 30 November 2020) <www.theguardian.com/environment/2020/nov/30/european-states-ordered-respond-youth-activists-climate-lawsuit>.
81 In *Bushfire Survivors for Climate Action Inc v Environment Protection Authority*, a group of survivors are arguing that the New South Wales Environment Protection Authority is in breach of its statutory duty under Chapter 2 of the *Protection of the Environment Operations Act 1997* (NSW), by failing to develop adequate climate policies. Following a November 2020 ruling, the group is permitted to present expert scientific evidence that will link climate change to bushfire risk (*Bushfire Survivors for Climate Action Inc v Environment Protection Authority* [2020] NSWLEC 152).
82 See 'The Youth Vs Clive Palmer's Waratah Mine', *Youth Verdict* (Post, 2020) <www.youthverdict.org.au/current-court-battles>.
83 Jeff Todd, 'A "Sense of Equity" in Environmental Justice Litigation' (2020) 44 *Harvard Environmental Law Review* 169, 174.
84 'Youth Activists Claim Clive Palmer's Proposed Coal Mine Could Breach Their Human Rights', *ABC 7.30 Report* (online, 13 May 2020) <www.abc.net.au/7.30/youth-activists-claim-clive-palmers-proposed-coal/12245602>.
85 *Waratah Coal Pty Ltd v Youth Verdict Ltd and Ors* [2020] QLC 33 [77].
86 Justine Bell-James and Briana Collins, 'Queensland's *Human Rights Act*: A New Frontier for Australian Climate Change Litigation?' (2020) 43(1) *University of New South Wales Law Journal* 3, 33–7.
87 Supreme Court of Victoria, 'Court Approves Distribution of Almost $700M in 2009 Black Saturday Bushfire Class Actions' (Media Release, 7 December 2016).
88 'Bushfire Class Action: Tree Falling on Endeavour Energy Power Line Sparked 2013 Blue Mountains Fire, Court Told', *ABC News* (online, 17 February 2016) <www.abc.net.au/news/2016-02-17/endeavour-energy-power-line-sparked-2013-blue-mountains-fire/7175634>.
89 'Victims Launch $150 Million Legal Class Action against SA Power Networks over Cudlee Creek Bushfire in Adelaide Hills', *ABC News* (online, 11 March 2021) <www.abc.net.au/news/2021-03-11/class-action-lawsuit-launched-over-cudlee-creek-bushfire/13236908>.
90 Gee and Anguiano (n 28) 37.
91 Ivan Penn, Peter Eavis and James Glanz, 'How PG&E Ignored Fire Risks in Favor of Profits', *The New York Times* (online, 18 March 2019) <www.nytimes.com/interactive/2019/03/18/business/pge-california-wildfires.html>.
92 Gee and Anguiano (n 28) 202.
93 Penn, Eavis and Glanz (n 91).
94 Ivan Penn and Peter Eavis, 'PG&E Pleads Guilty to 84 Counts of Manslaughter in Camp Fire Case', *The New York Times* (online, 16 June 2020) <www.nytimes.com/2020/06/16/business/energy-environment/pge-camp-fire-california-wildfires.html>.
95 Stephen Pyne, 'California Wildfires Signal the Arrival of a Planetary Fire Age', *The Conversation* (online, 11 September 2020) <https://theconversation.com/california-wildfires-signal-the-arrival-of-a-planetary-fire-age-125972>.

96 Ibid.
97 Gee and Anguiano (n 28) 205.
98 Ibid 207.
99 Quoted in ibid 208.
100 Carbon Majors are the corporations that produce fossil fuels and cement.
101 Richard Heede, 'Tracing Anthropogenic Carbon Dioxide and Methane Emissions to Fossil Fuel and Cement Producers, 1854–2010' (2014) 122 *Climatic Change* 229.
102 Matthew Taylor and Jonathan Watts, 'Revealed: The 20 Firms behind a Third of All Carbon Emissions', *The Guardian* (online, 9 October 2019) <www.theguardian.com/environment/2019/oct/09/revealed-20-firms-third-carbon-emissions>.
103 The case was stalled in 2020 by the onset of the pandemic, which prevented a planned inspection of the premises in Peru.
104 *City of Oakland v BP PLC* 325 FSupp3d 1017 (ND Cal 2018) 1023.
105 Peter Hannam, 'ACT Seeks Climate Litigation Advice as Court Action Gathers Momentum', *The Sydney Morning Herald* (online, 2 December 2018) <www.smh.com.au/environment/climate-change/act-climate-litigation-court-rattenbury-canberra-20181201-p50jk4.html>.
106 Taylor and Watts (n 102).
107 Jeremy Moss and Persephone Fraser, *Australia's Carbon Majors Report* (Report, Practical Justice Initiative, UNSW, 2019) 9.
108 Adam Morton, 'Australian Super Fund Agrees to Factor Climate Crisis into Decisions in "Groundbreaking" Case', *The Guardian* (online, 2 November 2020) <www.theguardian.com/australia-news/2020/nov/02/australian-super-fund-agrees-to-factor-climate-crisis-into-decisions-in-groundbreaking-case>.
109 Caroline Schelle, 'Aussie Law Student Katta O'Donnell Takes the Government to Court over Climate Change', *The Australian* (online, 10 November 2020) <www.theaustralian.com.au/breaking-news/aussie-law-student-katta-odonnell-takes-the-government-to-court-over-climate-change/news-story/7a4ee39e973be201361caf8989b7f730>
110 Kieran Pender, 'Suing for Climate Action: Can the Courts Save Us from the Black Hole of Political Inaction?', *The Guardian* (online, 15 November 2020) <www.theguardian.com/australia-news/2020/nov/15/suing-for-climate-action-can-the-courts-save-us-from-the-black-hole-of-political-inaction>.
111 'Bushfire Survivors and Friends of Earth's Response to Initial Assessment of ANZ Climate Complaint under OECD Guidelines', *Friends of the Earth Australia* (Post, 25 November 2020) <www.foe.org.au/bushfire_survivors_take_on_anz>.
112 Rob White and Ronald C Kramer, 'Critical Criminology and the Struggle against Climate Change Ecocide' (2015) 23 *Critical Criminology* 383, 393.
113 Danielle Celermajer, 'Omnicide: Who Is Responsible for the Gravest of All Crimes?', *ABC Religion and Ethics* (online, 3 January 2020) <www.abc.net.au/religion/danielle-celermajer-omnicide-gravest-of-all-crimes/11838534>.
114 Flanagan (n 32).
115 Paul Gregoire, 'Chomsky Declares "Morrison's Australia" amongst Top Three Climate Criminals', *Sydney Criminal Lawyers* (Post, 18 March 2020) <www.sydneycriminallawyers.com.au/blog/chomsky-declares-morrisons-australia-amongst-top-three-climate-criminals>.
116 Douglas Kahn, 'What Is an Ecopath?' (3 March 2020) *Sydney Review of Books* <https://sydneyreviewofbooks.com/essay/what-is-an-ecopath>.

117 See Anastacia Greene, 'The Campaign to Make Ecocide an International Crime: Quixotic Quest or Moral Imperative?' (2019) 30(3) *Fordham Environmental Law Review* 1, 2, 5–6.
118 Geert De Clercq, 'France's Macron Says Real "Ecocide" Going On in Amazon', *Reuters* (online, 24 August 2019) <www.reuters.com/article/us-g7-summit-amazon/frances-macron-says-real-ecocide-going-on-in-amazon-idUSKCN1VD2AM>.
119 'President Macron "Shares Ambition" to Establish International Crime of Ecocide', *Stop Ecocide* (Blog Post, 29 June 2020) <www.stopecocide.earth/press-releases-summary/president-macron-shares-ambition-to-establish-international-crime-of-ecocide>.
120 'France Plans to Jail "Ecocide" Offenders for 10 Years under New Laws', *Deutsche Welle* (online, 22 November 2020) <www.dw.com/en/france-plans-to-jail-ecocide-offenders-for-10-years-under-new-laws/a-55693750>.
121 Catherine Baksi, 'Work Begins on Legal Definition of "Ecocide"' (30 November 2020) *The Law Society Gazette* <www.lawgazette.co.uk/law/work-begins-on-legal-definition-of-ecocide/5106604.article>.
122 Eva Lövbrand, Malin Mobjörk and Rickard Söder, 'The Anthropocene and the Geo-Political Imagination: Re-Writing Earth as Political Space' (2020) 4 *Earth System Governance* 100051:1–8, 5.
123 Timothy Clark, *Ecocriticism on the Edge: The Anthropocene as a Threshold Concept* (Bloomsbury Publishing, 2015) 73.
124 Timothy Morton, *Dark Ecology: For a Logic of Future Coexistence* (Columbia University Press, 2016) 35.
125 Timothy Morton, *Hyperobjects: Philosophy and Ecology after the End of the World* (University of Minnesota Press, 2013) 136.
126 Morton (n 124) 45.
127 Ibid 9.
128 Ibid.
129 Beth Hill, 'Between Bushfire and Climate Change: Uncertainty, Silence and Anticipation Following the October 2013 Fires in the Blue Mountains, Australia' (PhD Thesis, The University of Sydney, 2017) 15.
130 Morton (n 124) 8.
131 See, eg, Colin Hickey and Ingrid Robeyns, 'Planetary Justice: What Can We Learn from Ethics and Political Philosophy?' (2020) 6 *Earth System Governance* 100045; John S Dryzek and Jonathan Pickering, *The Politics of the Anthropocene* (Oxford University Press, 2019) ch 4.
132 See Louis J Kotzé and Rakhyun E Kim, 'Earth System Law: The Juridical Dimensions of Earth System Governance' (2019) 1 *Earth System Governance* 100003.
133 Morton (n 124) 26.
134 Jacqueline Peel and Hari M Osofsky, 'A Rights Turn in Climate Change Litigation?' (2018) 7(1) *Transnational Environmental Law* 37.
135 One exception to this is the so-called *Future Generations* case, in which the personhood rights of the Amazon forest were recognised by the Colombian Supreme Court of Justice: see discussion in Alessandro Pelizzon, 'An Intergenerational Ecological Jurisprudence: The Supreme Court of Colombia and the Rights of the Amazon Rainforest' (2020) 2(1) *Law, Technology and Humans* 33.
136 Clark (n 123) 73

4 Narratives of activism

Nicole Rogers

Black Summer arrived at the end of a year distinguished by the global rise of two remarkable protest movements: that led by Extinction Rebellion and the youth climate strike movement. In 2019, large numbers of otherwise law-abiding citizens streamed on to the streets of cities around the world, obstructing traffic, staging mass die-ins and engaging in various acts of non-violent civil disobedience. Troupes of Red Rebels, with white faces and distinctive red robes, weaved their way in uncanny silence through public spaces. Pink boats appeared in London and Brisbane roads. Children and teenagers, inspired by the precise and uncompromising rhetoric of Swedish teenager Greta Thunberg, defied implied and explicitly stated expectations that they would leave all important decisions about their future to adults, and assembled in huge gatherings to give voice to their own fears. A growing number boycotted school every week as part of the Fridays For Future movement, sharing online images of themselves holding banners and placards outside politicians' offices and government buildings.

These movements appeared to signify something new: a pivotal moment in climate politics. Philip Alston, the United Nations Special Rapporteur on extreme poverty and human rights, singled out Extinction Rebellion and the school climate strikes as positive developments[1] in countering 'the natural complacency of governmental elites and vested interests of financial elites', and their capacity to 'sleep-[walk] towards catastrophe'.[2] Christiana Figueres and Tom Rivett-Carnac, leading players in international climate politics, endorsed both movements in a book released in early 2020,[3] and described civil disobedience as 'the most powerful way of shaping world politics'.[4] Bill McKibben[5] and Naomi Klein,[6] both experienced climate activists, welcomed the advent of the school strike movement and acknowledged the leadership role of Thunberg. The Collins dictionary chose the term 'climate strike' as its word of the year.[7]

Both movements were active in Australia during Black Summer, even as toxic air in smoke-infused cities and towns made outside gatherings

DOI: 10.4324/b22677-4

hazardous. There was a renewed desperation in public appeals for climate action. As the megafires continued to rage, it seemed that the movements, in conjunction with an unprecedented climate disaster, had achieved an unstoppable momentum; that public pressure on Australian governments to act decisively on climate mitigation would continue to build until it could no longer be disregarded. With the widespread implementation of pandemic restrictions in late March, however, the global landscape of protest was unexpectedly and dramatically altered.

In this chapter, I consider narratives of climate activism during 2020 and their intersection with what some commentators[8] consider to be the most prominent social movement of that year: the Black Lives Matter movement. In public spaces, in the digital arena and in courtrooms, climate activists continued to emphasise the urgency of acting on the climate emergency. Other emergencies intervened, however, to detract from the political impact of continuing protests and, as I outline in the final section of this chapter, judicial intolerance of arguments of climate emergency further impeded their efforts.

Protest during the megafires

The megafires commenced well before summer; by early September 2019, there were fires raging in hitherto unburnt areas of Queensland. Two global school climate strikes occurred subsequently, one later in September and the other in November. Contrasting images from the two Sydney strikes highlight the impact of the megafires on Australia's most densely populated city. In September, young speakers addressed packed crowds in Sydney's Domain under a clear blue sky. By November, as strikers amassed outside the Liberal Party's headquarters in Kings Cross to listen to an account of devastation and loss from teenage bushfire survivor Shiann Broderick, the sky had taken on the ominous, brownish hue that distinguished much of Black Summer, and many of the strikers wore face masks.

In late December, when young people gathered outside the Prime Minister's Kirribilli abode while he holidayed in Hawaii, smoke pollution was still at dangerous levels; undeterred by this, they were prepared to camp in the street until Morrison's return. They were moved on by the police, famously in the case of 13-year-old Izzy Raj-Seppings, whose tearful exchange with a police officer was filmed by a fellow activist. Footage of Raj-Seppings, defiantly raising her hand-lettered sign as she left the scene, went viral and transformed the teenager into one of the leaders of youth climate activism in Australia. Her sign read: 'Look at what you've left us. Watch us fight it. Watch us win'.[9]

In early December, Melinda Plesman travelled to Canberra with blackened remnants of her destroyed Nymboida house and, in a compelling one-woman protest, arranged them outside Parliament House; on a piece of corrugated iron, she had painted the words: 'Morrison, your climate crisis destroyed my home'.[10] Thousands attended an emergency climate change rally in Sydney on 11 December, following a day in which air pollution reached unprecedented levels.[11] Later that month, a Christmas-themed performance took place in Martin Place in the centre of the city, on yet another day of dangerous air quality. The arrival of six reindeer, a number of dead elves and a fake Prime Minister, masquerading as Santa Claus on a sleigh and scattering coal, led to two hours of traffic delays. A choir sang a version of 'Silent Night', with the substituted lyrics of 'Stop Coal Mining Now'.[12]

In early January, images of terrified fire refugees on beaches and in boats, of exhausted fire fighters and incinerated wildlife, propelled people on to the streets in large numbers to participate in mass rallies for climate justice. Thousands gathered again in Sydney, many wearing masks in a largely futile attempt to avoid the toxic air; for some, this was their first protest.[13] Rallies took place in the other capital cities and many regional towns. There were calls for the resignation of the Prime Minister. Around the world, outside Australian embassies, people assembled in solidarity.[14] At the end of January, a group of self-described 'quiet Australians' held a vigil in front of the office of federal Liberal politician David Sharma, in one of Sydney's wealthiest electorates; again, for many attendees and indeed the organisers, this was their first involvement in protest activities.[15]

While much ire was directed towards the federal government and its leader, News Corp, widely perceived as a prime disseminator of misinformation on the climate crisis, was also targeted by activists. A 'lie-in' protest, organised outside the Sydney News Corp offices, was designed to highlight the omissions and misleading statements circulated by the corporation's media outlets. Images of Brad Pedersen's initial solo lie-in were broadly circulated on social media; a subsequent protest at the end of January featured speakers, placards and approximately 400 people lying on the road. Pedersen expressed his reasoning thus: 'Why can't we lie outside Newscorp, when they lie all the time?'[16] A group of artists adopted an alternative tactic: removing advertising posters from bus shelters in Melbourne, Sydney and Brisbane, and replacing them with artwork highlighting the tragedy of the bushfires and the federal government's complicity. Contributors to such acts of 'Bushfire Brandalism' were also attempting to counter bias and misinformation in News Corp coverage of the fires.[17]

When the federal Parliament resumed sitting in Canberra in early February, a People's Climate Assembly took place on the lawns outside Parliament House, with participants urging the government to act on the climate emergency.[18] In mid-February, the Melbourne Town Hall was filled to capacity for a National Climate Emergency Summit. By then, the number of COVID-19 cases, in Australia and elsewhere, was beginning to escalate.

Pandemic climate activism

The World Health Organisation pandemic declaration in mid-March, and the flurry of regulatory responses that followed, had an immediate, chilling impact on climate activism. These measures put an end to large-scale, disruptive protests in public spaces, including those staged by school children. Participation in rallies and demonstrations now constituted a violation of new social codes of conduct and biosecurity regulatory measures. As Andreas Malm has put it, crowds, 'the fuel of every social movement', had 'suddenly become so insalubrious as to be outlawed'.[19] In at least two Australian jurisdictions, police would pre-emptively target protest organisers throughout the year, with arrests, threats and legal proceedings.[20] Climate activists, in Australia and elsewhere, were forced to reassess their commitment to ongoing disruption.

Greta Thunberg announced the digitalisation of the Fridays For Future movement in mid-March, tweeting that '[i]n a crisis we change our behaviour and adapt to the new circumstances for the greater good of society'.[21] An image of her iconic school strike sign, propped against a railing in front of the Swedish Parliament together with her jacket and shoes, subsequently appeared on her Instagram account.[22] Young people continued to strike at home on Fridays, posting online images of themselves with hand-lettered signs throughout 2020. The political efficacy of such school strikes was diminished during a period of widespread school closures. By mid-April, 191 countries had closed schools nationwide.[23] School closures would continue to occur, intermittently, throughout the year and beyond.

For the student organisers of the Australian Strike 4 Climate Action movement, as for school strikers elsewhere, the scaling down of their activities was a necessary but difficult adjustment; a mass strike planned for May was conducted online. Young people abandoned mass mobilisations in the public arena for the less visible, digital space. Australian Rebels also devised strategies of online activism. Extinction Rebellion Australia's digital rebellion, launched in May, was devised with four aims, the first of which was making mass mischief online. One hundred rebels were reported to have 'swarmed' every social media post made by Australia's four major banks, in order to highlight their funding of climate destruction. In responding to the approval of a coalmine under a major Sydney water reservoir, Rebels emailed and 'geo-blitzed' the New South Wales Environment Minister and Peabody Energy.[24]

Digital activism can be extremely effective; for instance, a campaign on the social media platform TikTok resulted in low numbers at President Trump's first pandemic rally in June 2020, after millions registered without any intention of attending.[25] In the same month, climate activists sent thousands of emails to global reinsurance company Aspen Re, asking the company to end its support for Adani's Carmichael mine; Aspen Re subsequently announced that it would not underwrite further work on the mine.[26] Nevertheless, one sociologist described digital activism as 'amplifying within an echo chamber'.[27] Twitter hashtags, she pointed out, lack the visibility of large crowds in the streets.[28]

Digital activism also lacks the performative impact of compelling image events, the centrality of which, as a key strategy for environmental activists, was highlighted by communication scholar Kevin Michael DeLuca in 1999. DeLuca acknowledged the transformative impact of image events that 'move[d] the meanings of fundamental ideographs',[29] such as progress and nature. The assumption of control over and blocking of roads, for instance, a key strategy for Extinction Rebellion and the school climate strikers, is both a literal and symbolic disruption of 'a major artery of industrialism'.[30] It is a gesture of defiance, a refusal to comply with the prevailing social code that privileges cars over people.[31] In his analysis, event is 'rupture which opens up truths'.[32] An example readily springs to mind: the image of a Swedish teenager with a hand-lettered sign, sitting outside the Swedish Parliament.

DeLuca argued that in a mediatised world, in which the focus is on spectacle and the spectacular, image events are a 'necessary tactic for oppositional politics';[33] in fact, images are far more powerful than dialogue.[34] Claudia Orenstein has similarly observed that 'the visible act of performance itself speaks far louder than any merely didactic argument'.[35] DeLuca's arguments retain their relevance even in a 'wildly transformed mediascape',[36] one which confers upon activists 'extraordinary, unprecedented world-changing power'[37] but simultaneously decouples humans from Earth.

Activists can face formidable obstacles in negotiating their terms of engagement with formal media organisations; DeLuca designated this terrain as 'enemy territory'.[38] This is less significant with the expansion and proliferation of alternative platforms in the twenty-first century. Social media outlets, despite compelling privacy and surveillance concerns, the dominance of algorithms and the enhanced potential for fake news, offer a levelling out, or democratisation, of media channels. Activist image events can be broadcast almost instantaneously on Instagram, Facebook, YouTube and other platforms, without overt moderation and editorial censorship.

Given the enduring importance of image events in an image-saturated virtual universe,[39] and their power, when utilised by activists, to 'interrupt and transform the taken-for-granted',[40] pandemic restrictions presented a significant challenge for climate and environmental activists. Performative interactions in public spaces took on a new and potentially deadly significance. As a dance critic observed, every 'movement has morals and consequences – its own choreographic score, or set of instructions – in this age of the coronavirus'.[41] Die-ins, for instance, intended to make clear the links between the climate crisis and mass deaths, 'raised the specter of contamination' much more directly than had the ACT UP die-ins of the 1980s:[42] police could contract or transmit a potentially deadly disease by attempting to discipline unruly bodies. Although many climate activists resolved such moral and legal dilemmas by confining their activities to the digital sphere, others found creative ways to engage in embodied protest and stage non-transgressive image events.

Pandemic image events

In Australia, such events included a yoga protest on the part of members of a local community, determined to save a last remnant of unburnt South Coast woodland from development; mats were appropriately distanced.[43] Collections of shoes were assembled in various public spaces around the world, including Australian cities,[44] conjuring up the Parisian shoe protest during COP21 in 2015. Extinction Rebellion activists staged a 'Now We're Cookin' With Gas' event outside the Goulburn office of the federal Energy Minister, with a simulacrum of the planet attached to a gas bottle and masked, costumed dancers.[45] A small group of masked young people gathered outside a Samsung shop in Sydney, threatening a youth boycott of its products if the corporation continued to support Adani's controversial Carmichael mine in the Galilee Basin in Queensland; shortly afterwards, Samsung Securities announced that it would no longer finance Adani's mining activities.[46] In late September, the School Strike 4 Climate Action movement staged over 600, socially distanced, yellow themed actions across Australia, rallying under the slogan of 'Fund Our Future Not Gas'.[47] This was part of a global day of COVID-compliant student strikes across the world.[48]

In October, during the so-called Spring Rebellion, five topless and masked Rebels, bodies painted in flames, glued themselves to the inside foyer windows of the Independent Planning Commission in protest against its approval of Santos's Narrabri coal seam gas project.[49] A bed appeared outside Parliament House in Sydney, with a masked couple enacting the intimate relationship between Santos and the New South Wales government.[50] These provocative performances followed an earlier protest in Adelaide, in August, when masked protesters chained themselves together in the lobby of Santos's headquarters.[51]

The depositing of a large pile of cow manure outside the Sydney office of News Corp, in front of a small, socially distanced gathering, was part of a global day of action in early September. The intention was to highlight the media corporation's role in disseminating misinformation on the climate crisis.[52] A socially distanced Dead Sea March in Hobart during October attracted approximately 150 people, and was followed by a die-in.[53] In November, Stop Adani activists targeted the Sydney Cricket Ground, where India was playing against Australia in the first match of the season; they gathered outside, with banners and mock stumps, objecting to a proposed loan to Adani by the State Bank of India.[54] Two enterprising protesters halted play when they ran on to the ground with their banners.[55]

None of these image events violated public health directions. Inventive performances by Rebels and school strikers elsewhere in the world throughout 2020, featuring props such as fake oil, fake blood, posters, the ubiquitous colourful banners and even a pink elk,[56] were also COVID-compliant. There was an overwhelming consensus amongst climate activists that it was necessary to obey such directions, despite their endorsement of mass civil disobedience and rule breaking. This socially responsible stance could be contrasted with the position adopted by participants in the anti-lockdown protests that erupted in various forms in Australia, particularly during the Melbourne lockdown, and around the world throughout 2020: namely, that pandemic restrictions constituted an unwarranted infringement of personal liberty and human rights, and should therefore be flouted.[57]

Given the dearth of active cases and minimal community transmission, pandemic restrictions had been gradually wound down throughout Australia by the end of 2020; this, of itself, created an additional dilemma for climate activists. The pandemic represented the most globally disruptive event in recent decades, one which triggered extraordinary emergency measures on the part of governments worldwide. It was difficult to see how activist strategies could compete with this level of disruption, or trigger this level of responsiveness by nation states. Furthermore, the activist goal of disruption was unlikely to attract popular support at a time when the overriding imperative was to restore some measure of financial and social stability. When two climate activists blocked traffic in Brisbane in December 2020, as part of a Defy Disaster week, the Brisbane Lord Mayor tweeted: 'Good morning to everyone except these clowns who want to disrupt the CBD while it's only just starting to recover from the economic impacts of COVID-19! #lockthemup'.[58]

While there were sound grounds for arguing that both the climate and pandemic crises, and the science behind them, should be acknowledged and addressed, the strategy of compliance adopted by Rebels and strikers throughout 2020 can be viewed as a tactical error. For these groups, the climate emergency eclipses all other emergencies; this emergency is the sixth mass extinction event that will annihilate humanity, together with countless other species. A global pandemic, despite its significant and rising death toll, cannot compete with this. The climate emergency is already killing people;[59] as a public health crisis itself, it overshadows COVID-19 in magnitude and impact. The reversion from rule-breaking to rule-following in 2020 detracted from the urgency of the climate emergency message. Without mass civil disobedience, climate activist movements lost much of their radical impact.

This was thrown into sharp relief when the Black Lives Matter protests erupted at the end of May, and crowds of protesters engaged in the mass gatherings prohibited under pandemic guidelines and restrictions. Large-scale street activism in 2020 was, it seemed, no longer dominated by awareness of the climate crisis.

Black Lives Matter and climate activism

On 25 May 2020, a black American man, George Floyd, died at the hands of a police officer on the streets of Minneapolis. Floyd's final, anguished minutes, as the officer knelt on his neck, were filmed by a bystander; the footage went viral. The death of Floyd proved to be the catalyst for global Black Lives Matter protests that could not be contained on the screens of a virtual, locked down world. Young and old, black and white, masked and unmasked, people flooded on to the streets despite the very real health risks of mass gatherings. In the United States alone, over 7750 demonstrations in over 2440 locations took place in the three months following Floyd's murder.[60]

In Australia, with its shameful history of black deaths in custody, thousands of people were spurred into action. It was a matter of priorities; as Aboriginal novelist Melissa Lucashenko wrote, 'everyone [at the protests] clearly understood that while COVID is *really, really serious, you mob*, the virus of racism is even more dangerous to Aboriginal bodies'.[61] The lethal emergency of racial injustice could no longer be disregarded. Police efforts to prevent the protests, which included court challenges[62] and arrests,[63] were seen as further evidence of the systemic racism behind the over-policing and over-incarceration of Aboriginal Australians. Resistance is fundamental to the political messaging of both the Extinction Rebellion and Black Lives Matter movements, but resistance generates disparate, racially discriminatory responses from the State.

In fact, the Australian rallies did not cause a spike in new infections. Although some commentators sought to find connections between the Melbourne demonstrations and a second wave of cases some weeks later, this claim was refuted by the Victorian health department.[64]

By way of contrast, in curtailing their own activities, climate activists conceded that the pandemic emergency should take precedence over the climate emergency, or at least be addressed with the same level of concern and care. The message from a COVID-compliant, youth protest in Berlin in April, spelt out in thousands of protest placards, was 'Fight Every Crisis';[65] the slogan was circulated as a key part of the online digital strike that accompanied the display,[66] and widely adopted by the climate strike movement.[67] As one 17-year-old Irish organiser put it, 'We are people who listen to the scientists and it would be hypocritical of us to not treat this as a crisis'.[68] Young people acknowledged an obligation of intergenerational care which, as one activist noted, deserved a reciprocal response from their elders.[69]

Fight every crisis

The injunction to fight every crisis applied not only to the pandemic. As the Black Lives Matter movement heightened global awareness of racial inequalities, climate activists in Australia and elsewhere accepted that racial justice is integral to climate justice.

Extinction Rebellion had already faced criticism in 2019 for its disregard for racial issues in promoting and encouraging mass arrests. Black and ethnic minority groups argued that this approach 'effectively made the protests the preserve of privileged white people'.[70] The Black Lives Matter movement brought this issue to the forefront. In July 2020, Extinction Rebellion released a statement in which it was acknowledged that 'our tactic of arrest has made it easier for people of privilege to participate and that our behaviours and attitudes fed into the system of white supremacy'. The movement apologised for the fact that 'this recognition comes so late'.[71]

In May 2019, in an open letter to Extinction Rebellion, dozens of groups collectively calling themselves 'the Wretched of the Earth' sought to remind the movement that, for many communities, 'the house has been on fire for a long time'; they wrote that 'the climate movement must reflect the complex realities of everyone's lives in their narrative'.[72] Generally, black climate activists have been denied the same level of participation and media coverage experienced by their white counterparts. Prominent Ugandan youth climate activist Vanessa Nakate was cropped out of a photograph, taken at a 2020 press conference, in which she appeared with four white youth activists; she subsequently spoke out about the erasure of climate activists of colour.[73] Indigenous people and those from the Global South have struggled to have their voices heard at United Nations climate change events.[74]

In promoting its September 2020 'rebellion', Extinction Rebellion UK acknowledged the 'intersection of global crises', encompassing the climate crisis, the pandemic, racial injustice and economic inequality.[75] Climate activists elsewhere also supported the Black Lives Matter movement, joining protests and emphasising the intersection between racial justice and climate justice.[76] Greta Thunberg pointed out that those who fight for climate justice cannot disregard the fact that, in many parts of the world, 'social and racial injustices have never been officially acknowledged'.[77] In an interview later in 2020, she made her position clear: 'Whatever is the issue, it's the fight for justice'.[78]

In Australia, organisers of the School Strike 4 Climate Australia Network were quick to respond to the Black Lives Matter movement, urging supporters to participate in Stop Black Deaths in Custody protests and pointing out that '[t]here is no climate justice without First Nations justice and Racial Justice'.[79] The interconnectedness of justice for First Nations people and climate justice was also emphasised by the Stop Adani network on their website.[80] Extinction Rebellion Sydney issued a statement of solidarity with the Black Lives Matter movement.[81]

Advocates for First Nations rights in Australia and climate activists have a common adversary in the mining industry. Judith Brett has pointed out that the industry, in contending with the climate movement, is deploying the same strategies developed to defeat Indigenous land rights in the 1990s.[82] The disregard by mining corporations for the cultural obligations and responsibilities of First Nations people was clearly apparent in a notorious incident in May 2020, when mining company Rio Tinto destroyed a 46,000-year-old sacred site at Juukan Gorge in Western Australia. The mining industry has persevered with projects in the face of resistance from First Nations people. Traditional owners have sought to prevent the Adani mine through a series of legal challenges[83] and protests; this has also been the case with the Shenhua Watermark coalmine.[84] In early December 2020, following the approval of Santos's Narrabri coal seam gas project by the federal Environment Minister, Gomeroi traditional owners and climate activists gathered together to protest against the mining operation.[85]

As previously discussed, some humanities scholars have objected to the species framing inherent in the Anthropocene narrative, in which humanity at large is identified as a geological agent and force, on the basis that this narrative conceals intra-species inequalities inherent in the origins of the fossil economy[86] and certainly apparent in present-day carbon footprints.[87] Malm and Holmberg, for instance, have argued that it is not possible to 'write off divisions between human beings as immaterial to the broader picture, for such divisions have been an integral part of fossil fuel combustion in the first place'.[88] An activist emphasis upon the integration of social justice and climate justice objectives is consistent with this stance, and with Chakrabarty's injunction to zoom both in and out. It resonates with the established tenets of social ecology, as pioneered by philosopher Murray Bookchin: in particular, the challenge to hierarchy 'as a stabilizing or ordering principle' in the realms of both natural ecosystems and human society.[89]

Throughout 2020, activist challenges to hierarchy emerged in yet another domain: the courtroom. Importantly, the campaign for judicial acknowledgement of the climate emergency could continue undeterred by pandemic restrictions on various forms of civil disobedience.

Climate activists in the courtroom

As climate change protest ramped up during 2019, Australian politicians resorted to disparaging rhetoric[90] and governments put forward legislation intended to deter protesters. In October 2019, in response to Extinction Rebellion protests that had created disruption in Brisbane, and protests against coal mining in north Queensland, the Queensland government passed the so-called dangerous attachment device laws;[91] under this legislation, the use of allegedly dangerous locking devices was punishable by a term of imprisonment of up to two years. In addition, police powers to search suspected activists were expanded. This constituted the latest addition to a growing arsenal of Australian anti-protest laws.[92]

In November that year, Prime Minister Scott Morrison identified 'a new breed of radical activism' that posed a threat to the future of mining in Australia, and indicated that the advocacy of boycotts against polluting companies would soon attract criminal penalties.[93] Shortly afterwards, seemingly undaunted by the 2017 High Court decision[94] in which the State's anti-protest legislation[95] had been struck down as unconstitutional, the Tasmanian lower house passed an amended version of the same Act;[96] the word 'protester' was deleted but heavy penalties for protest activities remained.

In 2020, as Australian climate activists explored novel ways to politicise the climate emergency during a pandemic, a number found themselves in court being prosecuted, and appealing convictions, for various offences relating to their protest activities. In some instances, they were successful. In August, a magistrate dismissed charges against David Shoebridge, a Greens politician, and others arrested during the December rally outside Kirribilli House.[97] Scott Ludlum, a former federal Greens politician, and 11 others also had charges dismissed;[98] they had been arrested for failing to move off a closed road during an approved climate rally in 2019, and given onerous bail conditions that were successfully contested at the time.[99] In Queensland, a District Court judge, acknowledging the relevance of the activists' political motivations and the excessiveness of the original sentence, set aside two of the first convictions under the State's dangerous attachment device law.[100] Eleanor Haas and Gali Schell utilised a 'dragon's den' device in January 2020 to temporarily halt operations on the coal-transporting Aurizon railway line in north Queensland. Of particular interest is the fact, as noted by the judge, that Haas 'was motivated to protest by, and the offending occurred in the context of, the bushfires in south eastern Australia'.[101]

Climate activist Greg Rolles was less successful in an attempt, in July 2020, to appeal his 2019 conviction.[102] Rolles had also blocked the Aurizon railway line, constructing a tripod over it in November 2018. He was the first climate activist to raise the extraordinary emergency defence in the Queensland *Criminal Code.*[103] In 2020, four other climate activists[104] invoked the same defence, a statutory version of the common law defence of necessity. Consequently, on several occasions throughout the year, judicial officers were required to reach conclusions on the nature of emergency, and the applicability of this emergency designation in the context of climate change. Furthermore, judges and magistrates had to adjudicate the fraught question of whether non-violent civil disobedience constitutes reasonable conduct on the part of ordinary citizens, who view the climate crisis as emergency and orthodox political channels as fundamentally flawed.

Law-breaking and the climate emergency

Kim Stanley Robinson's novel, *The Ministry for the Future*,[105] published in October 2020, is remarkable on a number of fronts: his concept of a Ministry charged with advocating for future human generations and 'all living creatures, past and present';[106] his wide-ranging discussion of plausible technological, economic and agricultural innovations; his emphasis on the key role of nation players such as China and India in facilitating global climate action; and his skillful interspersing of accounts of unnamed individuals and more-than-human entities in a fast-paced, engaging narrative. Importantly, in this futuristic vision, the causal factors for a dramatic transformation of world economies and the global use and supply of energy lie not only in the work of the Ministry, with its ceaseless negotiations, sponsoring of experiments and instigation of climate lawsuits, but, also, in law-breaking.

In the wake of a deadly heatwave in India, India breaks the terms of the *Paris Agreement* with a geoengineering experiment to release sulphur dioxide into the atmosphere.[107] More significantly, an ecoterrorist group which calls itself the Children of Kali is established with an absolute mandate: to kill those who refuse to change their ways.[108] In the years that follow, members of this group, other eco-terrorists[109] and an unofficial 'black wing'[110] of the Ministry carry out assassinations of oil executives;[111] hostage taking and attempted 're-education' of the economic elite;[112] targeted attacks on aircraft[113] and diesel-fuelled container ships;[114] mass infections of cattle[115] to discourage the production and consumption of meat; and the destruction of power plants.[116] A pivotal encounter between Frank May, sole survivor of the Indian heatwave, and head of the Ministry, Mary Murphy, contains the justificatory reasoning for law-breaking, even murder, to accelerate climate action: '[s]ome things might be against the law, but in that case *the law is wrong*'.[117] Frank elaborates upon the need for violent law-breaking:

> If you really were *from* the future, so that you knew for sure there were people walking the Earth today fighting change, so that they were killing your children and all their children, you'd defend your people. In defense of your home, your life, your people, you would kill an intruder.[118]

Mary, who increasingly sees herself as 'a harassed middle-aged female bureaucrat in a limp toothless international organization',[119] is persuaded by this exchange, conceding that 'the [legal] tools at our disposal are too weak'.[120]

Adherence to non-violence is a core precept of both the Extinction Rebellion and the school climate strike movements. Participants in both movements refuse to engage in any acts of violence, let alone acts on the scale of those deployed by the fictitious Children of Kali. This absolute refusal is viewed by some as a tactical error. In early 2021, Andreas Malm provided a sustained critique of this decision, presenting compelling arguments for the political efficacy of particular forms of targeted property destruction.[121] Malm himself was a member of a Swedish group of self-styled 'Indians of the Concrete Jungle', who committed minor acts of sabotage on SUVs in 2007.[122] Citing with approval the actions of climate activists Jessica Reznicek and Ruby Montoya, who vandalised the Dakota Access Pipeline,[123] as well as numerous historical antecedents,[124] Malm argued for the strategic disabling or dismantling of CO_2-emitting property and fossil fuel infrastructure such as pipelines.[125]

Despite the clear demarcation between violent and non-violent acts of climate resistance, the same justification for law-breaking, as articulated by Frank May, surfaces in relation to both categories: in emergency situations, when one is confronted with extreme danger, lawful actions and legal remedies may not suffice. This finds legal expression in the defence of necessity or, as it appears in some Australian jurisdictions,[126] the extraordinary emergency defence.

In the invocation of the climate emergency in support of their acts of civil disobedience, Australian climate activists are part of a growing international movement to establish non-violent law-breaking as a necessary response to the urgency of the climate crisis.

Climate activists and the extraordinary emergency defence

As previously stated, four climate activists, following the example of Greg Rolles in his 2019 trial, argued in 2020 in Queensland courtrooms that the extraordinary emergency of climate change justified law-breaking.

In a Northern Territory courtroom, two anti-fracking protesters, one of whom is a traditional owner of land threatened by fracking, raised climate change as an extraordinary emergency in their trial for charges of criminal damage.[127] The activists had drilled holes in the Northern Territory Parliamentary lawn in an attempt to attract political attention; they were acquitted on a technicality.[128]

Such arguments open an avenue for judicial findings of climate emergency. Magistrates and judges have, thus far, failed to take advantage of this opportunity. The magistrates' decisions in the Queensland trials, and the judgment of Queensland District Court Judge Rinaudo in Rolles's appeal, highlight gaps in judicial understanding of chronic, extraordinary emergencies. In light of such lacunae, activist attempts to frame climate change as emergency in a courtroom setting become problematic. Also problematic is the judicial assumption that what is reasonable equates, here, with what is lawful.

The extraordinary emergency defence is a statutory formulation of the common law defence of necessity, utilised with varying degrees of success by climate activists in trials in the United Kingdom,[129] the United States[130] and, recently, Switzerland.[131] The distinctive characteristic of the statutory defence is its wording: in Queensland, the trigger is a sudden *or* extraordinary emergency and this, arguably, is quite a different criterion to the imminent evil or harm that is one of the elements of the defence of necessity. Queensland judges and magistrates have, however, imported the notion of imminence into their reading of emergency.

In the 2019 trial of Greg Rolles, the presiding magistrate was prepared to conflate sudden and extraordinary, holding that a defendant must honestly believe on reasonable grounds that he or others were placed 'in sudden or imminent danger' in order to raise a section 25 defence.[132] The assumption of the arresting police officer, who stated that at the time there were no 'extraordinary emergencies that [he] could identify',[133] is also of interest here. On appeal, Judge Rinaudo similarly stressed the need for immediacy; he held that 'the emergency of climate change does not rise to the level of sudden or extraordinary' for the purpose of section 25, on the basis that no immediate action is required. In support of this reasoning, he pointed out that Rolles had been aware of climate change for over 30 years before engaging in his protest.[134] Emergency is interpreted here as exceptional, as limited in duration, as the not-normal. Chronic emergencies, emergencies which are not immediately apparent to a human observer at a particular point in time or in a particular location, are beyond the ambit of the defence.

This reasoning is not necessarily consistent with the Queensland Court of Appeal's interpretation of the defence in a decision pertaining to a drug offence, handed down in April 2020, although Judge Rinaudo cited this case.[135] Chief Justice Brown held that there was 'a temporal element imported' by the term emergency.[136] He also acknowledged, however, that an emergency 'may develop over time', citing rising floodwaters as an example; that an extraordinary emergency could be distinguished from a sudden emergency in this respect; and that the critical issue was whether it was 'of such a scale that it requires immediate action'.[137] It can be argued that climate change falls into this category, given its planetary dimensions and the scientifically supported imperative for immediate action, although this was not the approach adopted by Judge Rinaudo.

It was, also, not the position taken by Magistrate Walker in the trial of Tom Cotter in Emerald in August 2020. The climate emergency is ever present, ever intensifying, manifesting in an accelerating sequence of disasters, as Cotter made clear in his evidence; consequently, according to the magistrate, it was not a sudden or extraordinary emergency for the purpose of section 25. Of relevance for this magistrate was the fact that Cotter 'chose to take the action with deliberation in relation to a situation which he believes has been unfolding over a lengthy period of time, and which he believes to be increasing in severity'.[138]

The same magistrate refused to allow the evidence of Brendan Mackey, a renowned climate scientist, as to why climate change constitutes an extraordinary emergency. This, he held, was 'irrelevant and of no interest to the Court'; the question as to what constitutes an extraordinary emergency was a matter of law rather than fact.[139] In the trial of Rolles, Magistrate Muirhead permitted scientific evidence to be presented by the same scientist but discounted its significance, stating that it was not 'particularly helpful' in assisting the court in determining the relevant legal issues.[140]

Magistrate Gett, at the trial of three women who blocked a Brisbane road in August 2019, read section 25 differently, holding that an extraordinary emergency, for the purposes of the section, 'could be factual or the product of an honest and reasonable but mistaken belief'. In his view, the defendants' evidence, coupled with that provided by Professor Mackey, established that 'they each held an honest and reasonable belief in the existence of a climate emergency that was extraordinary'.[141] On the other hand, he reached the same conclusion as his fellow magistrates in finding that their actions could not be considered reasonable, and that their 'contention that their only resort left was to protest in the manner they did by blocking traffic, is untenable'.[142] Magistrate Muirhead and Magistrate Walker also emphasised the availability of lawful and legitimate avenues to 'advance [the activists'] legitimately held concerns'.[143]

The current judicial reading of the defence, in its application to climate activists in Queensland, raises a number of important concerns. Firstly, the finding that a determination as to the existence of an extraordinary emergency is a matter of law discounts the exhaustive body of scientific evidence that establishes climate change as an existential crisis for humanity and nonhuman species. The emergency status of climate change is a matter of scientific fact, not a matter for judicial determination. To suggest otherwise is to countenance the approach of United States Supreme Court Judge Amy Coney Barrett, who chose, in her confirmation hearings, to describe climate change as a 'very contentious matter of public debate' rather than as scientific fact.[144] For more than 70 climate and science journalists, and countless other observers, she thereby displayed 'a profound inability to understand the ecological crisis of our times'.[145]

Secondly, the current judicial reading of extraordinary emergency rests upon an assumption that emergencies are temporally and geographically contained. The planetary, temporally unlimited dimensions of the climate emergency take it outside this reading. The judicial findings are indicative of cognitive difficulties in understanding the scalar dimensions of the Anthropocene, and highlight the scalar limitations of the legal conceptual toolkit.

Finally, the assumption that lawful avenues for change suffice, in the context of the climate emergency, suggests a lack of understanding about the inadequacies of our political and legal structures in addressing climate change, and judicial misapprehension about the viability of the rule of law in a time of extraordinary emergency.

The multiple emergencies of 2020 and, in particular, new insights into the exigencies of chronic emergency may lead to a revision of the current, temporally limited, judicial reading of 'extraordinary emergency' in future trials. One salient feature of this particular discourse of emergency is that it emanates not from the executive arm of government, but from activists.

Emergency narratives from below

Carl Schmitt famously commenced his work *Political Theology* with the phrase: 'Sovereign is he who decides on the exception'.[146] The inherent danger in the broad acceptance of emergency as the 'new normal', and the consequential merger of the extraordinary and the ordinary, is the ensuing establishment, and legitimisation, of a permanent state of exception by the executive. In this section, I revisit my earlier discussion in Chapter 2 on managing emergency within a democratic rather than authoritarian framework, as part of a popular movement.

Giorgio Agamben embarks upon his seminal analysis of the state of exception, the 'no-man's-land between public law and political fact, and between the juridical order and life',[147] by referring to an ancient maxim: necessity has no law. The state of exception is based upon this maxim.[148] The interconnection between necessity and exception is important. Agamben's focus is on the imposition of the state of exception from above. At the outset, however, he notes that '[t]he problem of the state of exception presents clear analogies to that of the right of resistance'.[149] Underlying both 'is the question of the juridical significance of a sphere of action that is itself extrajuridical'.[150]

There are clear differences between the imposition of a state of exception, and popular uprisings and acts of resistance. Agamben's point is that both draw upon the same extra-legal rationale. By arguing necessity, either in its common law form or in the statutory version with its specific emphasis on emergency, climate activists seek judicial endorsement of their disregard for legal norms. Necessity here is the *popular* invocation of 'law's threshold or limit concept',[151] in contrast to the sovereign act of declaring a state of exception.

In taking this position, I am, in part, following the lead of political theorist Bonnie Honnig, who sought to highlight 'opportunities for democratic renewal' in emergency contexts.[152] It is possible, she argued, to conceive of 'a democratic state of exception'; the people can 'resist or affirm or call in all their plurality for the institution or end of a state of exception'.[153] It is arguable that an activist deployment of necessity, in its statutory or common law formulation, is one of the 'promising opportunities for democratizing and generating new sites of power even in emergency situations'[154] with which Honnig is concerned.

Declarations of emergency at executive level, also premised around arguments of necessity, lead to the setting aside of rights and freedoms and can imperil the rule of law. Judicial findings of emergency in activist trials, on the other hand, result not in wholesale abridgment of rights but, rather, in the setting aside of particular laws in specific situations in accordance with the slippery concept of justice; a concept which, as Derrida argued, lies beyond norms: 'the decision between just and unjust is never insured by a rule'.[155] The judge does this by conceding that the norm can never be an absolute. There is always the exception.

This process can be viewed as 're-judicializ[ing] the terrain'[156] of emergency. The defence is, potentially, a legal black hole, but it is also a safeguard. It protects the juridical order by incorporating concepts of necessity and emergency within that system, rather than consigning them to the executive arm of government as an arbitrary exercise of discretionary power and thereby imperilling the rule of law.

Conclusion

As with so many other human endeavours, climate activism underwent a seismic change throughout 2020. In a year ushered in by devastating, climate-charged megafires, thousands of Australians were compelled to protest for climate action on the part of their government. As the emergency of the fires was superseded by the pandemic emergency, activists responded to regulatory measures introduced to curb the spread of the virus. The school strike movement, adopting the motto of 'Fight Every Crisis', largely transferred its activities from street to screen. Extinction Rebellion devised creative tableaux which factored in masks and social distancing requirements. Such adjustments greatly reduced the radical, disruptive impact of both movements.

At the same time, Black Lives Matter protests in public spaces conveyed the sense of overriding urgency and defiance that had distinguished climate protests in 2019 and early 2020. Climate movements responded to the articulated emergency of racial injustice, acknowledging the inseparability of social justice and climate justice concerns. There was a growing recognition that multiple emergencies were interconnected at a fundamental level; this realisation reinforced the need for climate activists to zoom out *and* in, in devising strategies and goals.

In courtrooms, climate activists tested the parameters of anti-protest legislation, and sought judicial acknowledgement of the extraordinary emergency of climate change. In a year in which there was increasing scrutiny and discussion of executive overreach as a consequence of the pandemic, the activist pursuit of climate emergency declarations from the judiciary largely escaped notice. Nevertheless, such courtroom debates formed an integral part of evolving emergency discourses in 2020.

In the next chapter, I step back from my analysis of climate narratives in public fora, in courtrooms, and in online and other media channels. My focus in this final chapter is on the influence of the megafires upon fictitious texts and, more broadly, on how narrative framings and thematic content from climate and apocalyptic fiction anticipated and shaped our experience of the Black Summer megafires.

Notes

1 Philip Alston, *Climate Change and Poverty: Report of the Special Rapporteur on Extreme Poverty and Human Rights*, UN Doc A/HRC/41/39 (25 June 2019) 16.
2 Ibid 19.
3 Christiana Figueres and Tom Rivett-Carnac, *The Future We Choose: Surviving the Climate Crisis* (Manilla Press, 2020) 157, 158.
4 Ibid 158.
5 Bill McKibben, 'This Climate Strike Is Part of the Disruption We Need' (4 September 2019) *Yes! Magazine* <www.yesmagazine.org/opinion/2019/09/04/climate-strike-bill-mckibben-young-people>.
6 Klein has described Greta Thunberg as 'one of the great truth-tellers of this or any time': quoted in Lucy Diavolo, 'Greta Thunberg Wants You – Yes, You – to Join the Climate Strike' (16 September 2019) *Teen Vogue* <www.teenvogue.com/story/greta-thunberg-climate-strike-teen-vogue-special-issue-cover>.

7 Johanne Elster Hanson, '"Climate Strike" Named 2019 Word of the Year by Collins Dictionary', *The Guardian* (online, 7 November 2019) <www.theguardian.com/books/2019/nov/07/climate-strike-named-2019-word-of-the-year-by-collins-dictionary>.
8 See, eg, Nadya Tolokonnikova, 'A Year of Radical Political Imagination', *The New York Times* (online, 9 December 2020) <www.nytimes.com/2020/12/09/opinion/george-floyd-social-justice-pussy-riot.html>. In 2021, the Black Lives Matter movement was nominated for the Nobel peace prize by a Norwegian politician.
9 Isolde Raj-Seppings, 'I'm the 13-Year-Old Police Threatened to Arrest at the Kirribilli House Protest: This Is Why I Did It', *The Guardian* (online, 21 December 2020) <www.theguardian.com/australia-news/commentisfree/2019/dec/21/im-the-13-year-old-police-threatened-to-arrest-at-the-kirribilli-house-protest-this-is-why-i-did-it>.
10 'Woman Brings Remains of Home Lost in NSW Bushfires to Parliament in Climate Protest', *The Guardian* (online, 2 December 2019) <www.theguardian.com/australia-news/2019/dec/02/woman-brings-remains-of-home-lost-in-nsw-bushfires-to-parliament-in-climate-protest>.
11 Naaman Zhou, 'Sydney Climate Protest: Thousands Rally against Inaction amid Bushfire and Air Quality Crisis', *The Guardian* (online, 11 December 2019) <www.theguardian.com/environment/2019/dec/11/sydney-climate-protest-thousands-rally-against-inaction-amid-bushfire-and-air-quality-crisis>.
12 Paul Gregoire, 'Climate Activists Bring Sydney Traffic to a Standstill', *Sydney Criminal Lawyers* (Blog Post, 20 December 2019) <www.sydneycriminallawyers.com.au/blog/climate-activists-bring-sydney-traffic-to-a-standstill>.
13 'Bushfire Emergency Leads Thousands to Protest against PM and Climate Change Policies', *ABC News* (online, 10 January 2020) <www.abc.net.au/news/2020-01-10/bushfires-australia-protests-nationwide-sack-pm-scott-morrison/11857556>.
14 Bridget Brennan and Roscoe Whalan, 'Climate Action Protesters Angry over Australia's Bushfires Rally across Europe', *ABC News* (online, 11 January 2020) <www.abc.net.au/news/2020-01-11/scott-morrison-labelled-laughing-stock-europe-climate-protests/11859988>.
15 Tracy Bowden, 'Quiet Australians Decide It Is Time to Speak Up on Climate Change Action', *ABC News* (online, 29 January 2020) <www.abc.net.au/news/2020-01-29/new-activists-quiet-australians-government-action-climate-change/11903728>.
16 Paul Gregoire, '"They Lie All the Time": An Interview with the News Corp Lie-In's Brad Pedersen', *Sydney Criminal Lawyers* (Blog Post, 4 February 2020) <www.sydneycriminallawyers.com.au/blog/they-lie-all-the-time-an-interview-with-the-news-corp-lie-ins-brad-pedersen>.
17 Jenny Valentish, '"Australia's Largest Unsanctioned Art Show": Guerilla Bushfire Campaign Hijacks Bus Shelters', *The Guardian* (online, 4 February 2020) <www.theguardian.com/artanddesign/2020/feb/04/bushfire-brandalism-australian-artists-replace-bus-shelter-ads-with-political-posters>.
18 Graeme Dunstan, 'People's Climate Assembly Calls for Action', *The Echo* (online, 20 February 2020) <www.echo.net.au/2020/02/peoples-climate-assembly-calls-for-action>.
19 Andreas Malm, *How to Blow Up a Pipeline* (Verso, 2021) 2.

20 Louise Boon-Kuo et al, 'Policing Biosecurity: Police Enforcement of Special Measures in New South Wales and Victoria during the COVID-19 Pandemic' (2020) *Current Issues in Criminal Justice*:1–13, 7–8 <https://doi.org/10.1080/10345329.2020.1850144>.

21 Andrea Germanos, '"Coronavirus Isn't Stopping Us!": Youth Activists Adapt to Global Pandemic with Digital #ClimateStrikeOnline' (13 March 2020) *Common Dreams* <www.commondreams.org/news/2020/03/13/coronavirus-isnt-stopping-us-youth-activists-adapt-global-pandemic-digital>.

22 Barbara Miller, 'Coronavirus Sees Climate Kids Go from Protests Involving Hundreds of Thousands to Campaigning from Their Bedrooms', *ABC News* (online, 15 May 2020) <www.abc.net.au/news/2020-05-15/climate-kids-organise-protest-from-home-during-coronavirus/12244112>.

23 'COVID-19 and Human Rights: We Are All in This Together' (United Nations Secretary-General's Policy Brief, April 2020) 5 <www.un.org/sites/un2.un.org/files/un_policy_brief_on_human_rights_and_covid_23_april_2020.pdf>.

24 'Digital Rebellion May 2020', *Extinction Rebellion Australia* (Blog Post) <https://ausrebellion.earth/get-involved/digital-rebellion>.

25 Joanne Orlando, 'Teens Acting Fast and Strategically on Social Media to Get Political Messages Across', *The Sydney Morning Herald* (online, 24 June 2020) <www.smh.com.au/national/teens-acting-fast-and-strategically-on-social-media-to-get-political-messages-across-20200623-p5559q.html>.

26 Charlotte Grieve, 'Aspen Re Rules Out Insuring Adani Mine', *The Sydney Morning Herald* (online, 19 June 2020) <www.smh.com.au/business/banking-and-finance/aspen-re-rules-out-insuring-adani-mine-20200619-p5547s.html>.

27 Quoted in Shola Lawai, 'Coronavirus Halts Street Protests, But Climate Activists Have a Plan', *The New York Times* (online, 19 March 2020) <www.nytimes.com/2020/03/19/climate/coronavirus-online-climate-protests.html>.

28 Ibid.

29 Kevin Michael DeLuca, *Image Politics: The New Rhetoric of Environmental Activism* (Guilford Press, 1999) 52.

30 Ibid 161.

31 Ibid 162.

32 Kevin Michael DeLuca, 'Image Events Amidst Eco-Ruins: Social Media and the Mediated Earth' (2019) 16(4) *Communication and Critical/Cultural Studies* 329, 335.

33 DeLuca (n 29) 92.

34 Ibid 120.

35 Claudia Orenstein, 'Agitational Performance, Now and Then' (2001) 31 *Theater* 139, 151.

36 DeLuca (n 32) 329.

37 Ibid 332.

38 DeLuca (n 29) 87.

39 See Joshua Trey Barnett, 'Irrational Hope, Phenological Writing, and the Prospects of Earthly Existence' (2019) 16(4) *Communication and Critical/Cultural Studies* 382, 385.

40 Ibid 386.

41 Gia Kourlas, 'How We Use Our Bodies to Navigate a Pandemic', *The New York Times* (online, 31 March 2020) <www.nytimes.com/2020/03/31/arts/dance/choreographing-the-street-coronavirus.html>.

42 Susan Leigh Foster discusses this feature of ACT UP die-ins in 'Choreographies of Protest' (2003) 55(3) *Theatre Journal* 395, 404.

43 Laura Chung and Peter Hannam, 'Residents Protest to Save Unburnt Forest from Developer', *The Sydney Morning Herald* (online, 5 May 2020) <www.smh.com.au/national/nsw/residents-protest-to-save-unburnt-forest-from-developer-20200504-p54pmz.html>.

44 See, eg, Lucy Stone, 'Hundreds of Children's Shoes Laid Out in Silent Brisbane Climate Protest', *Brisbane Times* (online, 11 July 2020) <www.brisbanetimes.com.au/national/queensland/hundreds-of-children-s-shoes-laid-out-in-silent-climate-protest-20200711-p55b52.html>; Lucy Mae Beers, 'Extinction Rebellion Protests Planned in Melbourne This Weekend', *7News* (online, 19 June 2020) <https://7news.com.au/news/climate-change/extinction-rebellion-protests-planned-in-melbourne-this-weekend-c-1111552>.

45 'Please Proceed to Emergency Exits: Global Newsletter #41', *Extinction Rebellion* (Blog Post, 16 July 2020) <https://rebellion.global/blog/2020/07/16/newsletter-41>.

46 Graham Readfearn, 'Samsung Securities Pledges No Further Financial Backing for Adani Coal after Protest', *The Guardian* (online, 17 July 2020) <www.theguardian.com/business/2020/jul/17/samsung-securities-pledges-no-further-financial-backing-for-adani-coal-after-protest>.

47 'Global School Strike for Climate Change Movement Resumes, with Protests Taking Place across Australia', *ABC News* (online, 25 September 2020) <www.abc.net.au/news/2020-09-25/global-student-strike-for-climate-action/12702434>.

48 Fiona Harvey, 'Young People Resume Global Climate Strikes Calling for Urgent Action', *The Guardian* (online, 25 September 2020) <www.theguardian.com/environment/2020/sep/25/young-people-resume-global-climate-strikes-calling-urgent-action-greta-thunberg>.

49 AJ Tennant, 'Extinction Rebellion Tells Naked Truth at NSW Independent Planning Commission' (14 October 2020, Issue 1285) *Green Left Weekly* <www.greenleft.org.au/content/extinction-rebellion-tells-naked-truth-nsw-independent-planning-commission>.

50 Paul Gregoire, 'Get the Hell Out of Bed with Santos, Gladys, Warns Extinction Rebellion', *Sydney Criminal Lawyers* (Blog Post, 16 October 2020) <www.sydneycriminallawyers.com.au/blog/get-the-hell-out-of-bed-with-santos-gladys-warns-extinction-rebellion>.

51 'XR Unchained 17', *Extinction Rebellion* (Blog Post, 23 August 2020) <https://extinctionrebellion.uk/2020/08/23/xr-unchained-17>.

52 Paul Gregoire, 'Quit the Bullshit and Tell the Truth News Corp, Demands Extinction Rebellion', *Sydney Criminal Lawyers* (Blog Post, 5 September 2020) <www.sydneycriminallawyers.com.au/blog/quit-the-bullshit-and-tell-the-truth-news-corp-demands-extinction-rebellion>.

53 Christopher Ham, 'Police Arrest 27 Extinction Rebellion Protesters in Hobart Following Dead Sea March', *ABC News* (online, 3 October 2020) <www.abc.net.au/news/2020-10-03/police-arrest-27-extinction-rebellion-protesters-in-hobart/12729488>.

54 Jim McIlroy and Coral Wynter, 'Stop Adani Message Goes Down Well at the Cricket' (30 November 2020, Issue 1291) *Green Left Weekly* <www.greenleft.org.au/content/stop-adani-message-goes-down-well-cricket>.

55 Ibid.

56 See 'Rolling Rebellion. Global Newsletter 43', *Extinction Rebellion* (Blog Post, 8 September 2020) <https://extinctionrebellion.uk/2020/09/08/rolling-rebellion-global-newsletter-43>.

57 Danielle Celermajer and Dalia Nassar have argued, however, that in contrast to the emphasis on individual freedoms in anti-lockdown demonstrations in the United States, the protests in Germany stemmed from 'a concern for the well-being of the social whole': Danielle Celermajer and Dalia Nassar, 'COVID and the Era of Emergencies: What Type of Freedom Is at Stake?' (2020) 7(2) *Democratic Theory* 12, 16.

58 Quoted in Toby Crockford, 'Extinction Rebellion's Blockade of Edward Street in Brisbane CBD Ends', *Brisbane Times* (online, 7 December 2020) <www.brisbanetimes.com.au/national/queensland/extinction-rebellion-truck-blocks-edward-street-in-brisbane-cbd-20201207-p56l5f.html>.

59 See Paddy Manning, *Body Count: How Climate Change Is Killing Us* (Simon and Schuster, 2020).

60 Roudabeh Kishi and Sam Jones, *Demonstrations and Political Violence in America: New Data for Summer 2020* (Report, Armed Conflict Location and Event Data Project (ACLED), September 2020) 2 <https://acleddata.com/acleddatanew/wp-content/uploads/2020/09/ACLED_USDataReview_Sum2020_SeptWebPDF.pdf>.

61 Melissa Lucashenko, 'Too Deadly: Coronavirus in Black Australia' in Sophie Cunningham (ed), *Fire, Flood and Plague: Australian Writers Respond to 2020* (Vintage Books, 2020) 135, 142–3 (emphasis in original).

62 See, eg, *Commissioner of Police v Bassi* [2020] NSWSC 710, overturned on appeal in *Bassi v Commissioner of Police* [2020] NSWCA 109; *Commissioner of Police v Gray* [2020] NSWSC 867.

63 Naaman Zhou, 'Six Arrested at Sydney Black Lives Matter Protest as Dungay Family Deliver Petition to Parliament', *The Guardian* (online, 28 July 2020) <www.theguardian.com/australia-news/2020/jul/28/six-arrested-at-sydney-black-lives-matter-protest-as-dungay-family-deliver-petition-to-parliament>.

64 Amanda Meade, 'Black Lives Matter Protests, a Covid-19 Outbreak and the "Link" That Didn't Exist', *The Guardian* (online, 17 July 2020) <www.theguardian.com/media/2020/jul/17/black-lives-matter-protests-a-covid-19-outbreak-and-the-link-that-didnt-exist>.

65 '#FightEveryCrisis: Biggest Digital Demonstration Ever and Climate Strikes around the World', *Fridays For Future DE* (Blog Post, 25 April 2020) <https://fridaysforfuture.de/2404-en>.

66 Jeanette Cwienk, 'Climate Strikers Get Inventive during the COVID-19 Crisis', *Deutsche Welle* (online, 24 April 2020) <www.dw.com/en/climate-strikers-get-inventive-during-the-covid-19-crisis-fridays-for-future/a-53229262>.

67 Miller (n 22).

68 Quoted in Lawai (n 27).

69 In the words of one young Greek climate activist, 'Today we young people save the elderly by not going out to protest. Tomorrow the elderly must save my generation by taking it to the streets with us': quoted in Tim Schauenberg and Chetna Krishna, 'Tough Times ahead for Climate Protesters during Corona Pandemic', *Deutsche Welle* (online, 2 April 2020) <www.dw.com/en/tough-times-ahead-for-climate-protesters-during-corona-pandemic/a-52978469>.

70 Matthew Taylor, 'The Evolution of Extinction Rebellion', *The Guardian* (online, 4 August 2020) <www.theguardian.com/environment/2020/aug/04/evolution-of-extinction-rebellion-climate-emergency-protest-coronavirus-pandemic>.
71 Quoted in ibid.
72 Wretched of The Earth, 'An Open Letter to Extinction Rebellion' (4 May 2019) *Common Dreams* <www.commondreams.org/views/2019/05/04/open-letter-extinction-rebellion>.
73 Kenya Evelyn, '"Like I Wasn't There": Climate Activist Vanessa Nakate on Being Erased from a Movement', *The Guardian* (online, 29 January 2020) <www.theguardian.com/world/2020/jan/29/vanessa-nakate-interview-climate-activism-cropped-photo-davos>.
74 See Corrie Grosse and Brigid Mark, 'A Colonized COP: Indigenous Exclusion and Youth Climate Justice Activism at the United Nations Climate Change Negotiations' (2020) 11 *Journal of Human Rights and the Environment* 146.
75 @XRebellionUK (Extinction Rebellion UK) (Twitter, 3 July 2020, 9.30pm) <https://twitter.com/XRebellionUK/status/1279014643374198789>.
76 Ilana Cohen et al, 'As Protests Rage over George Floyd's Death, Climate Activists Embrace Racial Justice', *Inside Climate News* (online, 3 June 2020) <https://insideclimatenews.org/news/02062020/george-floyd-racial-justice-police-brutality-environment-climate-activism>; Lauren Aratani, 'With Big Rallies Cancelled, Young Climate Activists Are Adapting Election Tactics', *The Guardian* (online, 3 August 2020) <www.theguardian.com/us-news/2020/aug/03/young-climate-activists-rallies-us-elections-coronavirus>.
77 Greta Thunberg, 'Six Months on a Planet in Crisis: Greta Thunberg's Travel Diary from the US to Davos' (10 July 2020) *Time* <https://time.com/5863684/greta-thunberg-diary-climate-crisis>.
78 Oliver Whang, 'Greta Thunberg Reflects on Living through Multiple Crises in a "Post-Truth Society"' (29 October 2020) *National Geographic* <www.nationalgeographic.com/environment/2020/10/greta-thunberg-reflects-on-living-through-multiple-crises-post-truth-society>.
79 *School Strike 4 Climate* (Facebook Post, 1 June 2020) <www.facebook.com/StrikeClimate/posts/745929586236089>.
80 'Stand with #BlackLivesMatter and the Fight to Stop Black Deaths in Custody', *#StopAdani* (Post) <www.stopadani.com/solidarity_blm>.
81 Extinction Rebellion Sydney, 'Public Statement in Support of "Stop All Black Deaths in Custody: Solidarity with Long Bay Prisoners" Protest, 6.30pm Friday 12 June 2020' (Facebook Post, 12 June 2020) <www.facebook.com/xrsydney/posts/extinction-rebellion-sydney-stands-in-solidarity-with-the-black-lives-matter-mov/711602376077120>.
82 Judith Brett, 'The Coal Curse: Resources, Climate and Australia's Future' (June 2020, Issue 78) *Quarterly Essay* 46.
83 See Ben Smee, 'Adani Land-Use Agreement: Court Dismisses Indigenous Group's Appeal', *The Guardian* (online, 12 July 2019) <www.theguardian.com/environment/2019/jul/12/adani-land-use-agreement-court-dismisses-indigenous-groups-appeal>.
84 See, eg, *Talbott v Minister for the Environment* [2020] FCA 1042.
85 Lorena Allam, 'Hundreds Rally in Australian Capital Cities against the $3.6bn Narrabri Gas Project', *The Guardian* (online, 3 December 2020) <www.theguardian.com/australia-news/2020/dec/03/hundreds-rally-in-australian-capital-cities-against-the-36bn-narrabri-gas-project>.

86 Andreas Malm and Alf Hornborg, 'The Geology of Mankind? A Critique of the Anthropocene Narrative' (2014) 1(1) *The Anthropocene Review* 62, 63.

87 Ibid 64.

88 Ibid 66.

89 Murray Bookchin, *The Ecology of Freedom: The Emergence and Dissolution of Hierarchy* (Black Rose Books, rev ed, 1991) 37.

90 See examples of such rhetoric in Piero Moraro, 'Cattle Prods and Welfare Cuts: Mounting Threats to Extinction Rebellion Show Demands Are Being Heard, But Ignored', *The Conversation* (online, 11 October 2019) <https://theconversation.com/cattle-prods-and-welfare-cuts-mounting-threats-to-extinction-rebellion-show-demands-are-being-heard-but-ignored-124990>.

91 *Summary Offences and Other Legislation Amendment Act 2019* (Qu).

92 These include the *Summary Offences and Sentencing Amendment Act 2014* (Vic), *Workplaces (Protection from Protesters) Act 2014* (Tas), *Inclosed Lands, Crimes and Law Enforcement Amendment (Interference) Act 2016* (NSW), *Crown Land Management Regulation 2018* (NSW) and Criminal Code Amendment (Prevention of Lawful Activity) Bill 2015 (WA).

93 Paul Karp, 'Scott Morrison Threatens Crackdown on Protesters Who Would "Deny Liberty"', *The Guardian* (online, 1 November 2019) <www.theguardian.com/australia-news/2019/nov/01/scott-morrison-threatens-crackdown-on-secondary-boycotts-of-mining-companies>.

94 *Brown v Tasmania* (2017) 261 CLR 328.

95 *Workplaces (Protection from Protesters) Act 2014* (Tas).

96 Workplaces (Protection from Protesters) Amendment Bill 2019 (Tas); the Bill was defeated in the Legislative Council in March 2021.

97 Gus McCubbing, 'NSW Greens MP's Charge Dismissed by Court', *The Canberra Times* (online, 28 August 2020) <www.canberratimes.com.au/story/6900798/nsw-greens-mps-charge-dismissed-by-court>.

98 Joanna Panagopoulos, 'Extinction Rebellion Activists Cleared after Sydney Protest Arrest', *The Daily Telegraph* (online, 13 October 2020) <www.dailytelegraph.com.au/newslocal/central-sydney/extinction-rebellion-activists-cleared-after-sydney-protest-arrest/news-story/01b5939a275cc4d23499293efe31d096>.

99 Naaman Zhou, 'Extinction Rebellion: Scott Ludlum Has "Absurd" Bail Conditions Dismissed by Judge', *The Guardian* (online, 10 October 2019) <www.theguardian.com/environment/2019/oct/10/extinction-rebellion-scott-ludlam-has-absurd-bail-conditions-dismissed-by-judge>.

100 *EH v Queensland Police Service; GS v Queensland Police Service* [2020] QDC 205.

101 Ibid [25].

102 *Rolles v Commissioner of Police* [2020] QDC 331.

103 Section 25 of the *Criminal Code 1899* (Qu) states that: Subject to the express provisions of this Code relating to acts done upon compulsion or provocation or in self-defence, a person is not criminally responsible for an act or omission done or made under such circumstances of sudden or extraordinary emergency that an ordinary person possessing ordinary power of self-control could not reasonably be expected to act otherwise.

104 The combined trials of Emma Dorge, Clancey Maher and Holly Porter took place in Brisbane in March 2020; the magistrate handed down his decision at the end of June. Tom Cotter's trial took place in August in Emerald. The magistrate's findings were handed down in the same month.

105 Kim Stanley Robinson, *The Ministry for the Future* (Orbit, 2020).
106 Ibid 16.
107 Ibid 18–9.
108 Ibid 49.
109 Ibid 368.
110 Ibid 110, 546.
111 Ibid 135–7.
112 Ibid 160–4.
113 Ibid 228.
114 Ibid 229.
115 Ibid.
116 Ibid 230.
117 Ibid 99 (emphasis in original).
118 Ibid 100 (emphasis in original).
119 Ibid 241.
120 Ibid 109.
121 Malm (n 19).
122 Ibid 79–84.
123 Ibid 97–100.
124 Ibid 39–53.
125 Ibid 68–9, 70–5.
126 An extraordinary emergency statutory defence exists in some other Australian jurisdictions: see section 10.3 of the Commonwealth Criminal Code in Schedule 3 of the *Criminal Act 1995* (Cth); *Criminal Code Act 2002* (ACT) s 41; section 43BC of the Criminal Code of the Northern Territory of Australia (Schedule 1 of the *Criminal Code Act 1983* (NT)); *Crimes Act 1958* (Vic) s 322R; section 25 of the Western Australian Criminal Code (Schedule, *Criminal Code Act Compilation Act 1913* (WA)). In other Australian jurisdictions, the defence of necessity has not been codified and remains a common law defence.
127 Sarah Matthews, 'Protesters Who Drilled Holes in Parliament Lawns Had "Exhausted all Other Options", Court Hears', *NT News* (online, 19 October 2020) <www.ntnews.com.au/truecrimeaustralia/police-courts/protesters-who-drilled-holes-in-parliament-lawns-had-exhausted-all-other-options-court-hears/news-story/91de853842b040026c34111fa43abd6d>.
128 Sowaibah Hanifie, 'Darwin Judge Finds Anti-Fracking Protesters Not Guilty of Damaging Lawns outside NT Parliament', *ABC News* (online, 10 November 2020) <www.abc.net.au/news/2020-11-10/nt-fracking-protestors-who-drilled-holes-lawns-found-not-guilty/12867700>.
129 The Kingsnorth Six successfully utilised a statutory version of necessity in their 2008 trial, as did Roger Hallam, co-founder of Extinction Rebellion, and a colleague in their 2019 trial. Other attempts to raise necessity by climate activists in the United Kingdom have been unsuccessful. See discussion in Nicole Rogers, 'Climate Activism and the Extraordinary Emergency Defence' (2020) 94 *Australian Law Journal* 217, 224–5; Nicole Rogers, 'Beyond Reason: Activism and Law in a Time of Climate Change' (2018) 12(2) *Journal for the Study of Radicalism* 157, 171, 174.
130 Rogers 'Beyond Reason' (n 129) 171–3; Lance N Long and Ted Hamilton, 'The Climate Necessity Defense: Proof and Judicial Error in Climate Protest Cases' (2018) 38 *Stanford Environmental Law Journal* 57.
131 In January 2020, a Swiss judge acquitted 12 climate activists on the basis of necessity; they had played tennis, in a Credit Suisse branch, to draw attention

to the bank's fossil fuel investments. The prosecutor successfully appealed this decision in the Vaud Cantonal Court. See Emma Farge, 'Swiss Appeals Court Reverses Acquittal of Credit Suisse Climate Protesters', *Reuters* (online, 24 September 2020) <https://in.reuters.com/article/us-climate-change-trial/swiss-appeals-court-reverses-acquittal-of-credit-suisse-climate-protesters-idINKCN26F19G>.

132 *Police v Rolles* (Bowen Magistrates Court, MAG-00225465/18(5), 28 May 2019), unpublished decision, 3.

133 *Police v Rolles* (Bowen Magistrates Court, MAG-00225465/18(5), 16 May 2019), transcript, 20.

134 *Rolles v Commissioner of Police* [2020] QDC 331 [40].

135 Ibid [35]-[38].

136 *R v Dimitropoulos* [2020] QCA 75 [62] (Brown J).

137 Ibid.

138 *Police v Cotter* (Emerald Magistrates Court, MAG-00009515/20(8), 18 August 2020), unpublished decision, 4–5.

139 Ibid 2.

140 *Police v Rolles* (n 132) 2.

141 *Police v Dorge, Maher and Porter* (Brisbane Magistrates Court, MAG-00147905/19(0); MAG-00191578/19(8); MAG-00147866/19(4); MAG 00147966/19(9), 26 June 2020), unpublished decision, 16–7.

142 Ibid 17.

143 *Police v Cotter* (n 138) 5; *Police v Rolles* (n 132) 5.

144 Justin Novel and Antonia Juhasz, 'More Than 70 Climate and Science Journalists Challenge Supreme Court Nomination of Amy Coney Barrett' (25 October 2020) *Rolling Stone* <www.rollingstone.com/politics/political-commentary/amy-coney-barrett-climate-journalists-challenge-supreme-court-nomination-1080453>.

145 Ibid.

146 Carl Schmitt, *Political Theology: Four Chapters on the Concept of Sovereignty*, tr George Schwab (MIT Press, 1985) 5.

147 Giorgio Agamben, *State of Exception*, tr Kevin Attell (University of Chicago Press, 2005) 1.

148 Ibid.

149 Ibid 10.

150 Ibid 11.

151 Ibid 4.

152 Bonnie Honig, *Emergency Politics: Paradox, Law, Democracy* (Princeton University Press, 2009) xv.

153 Ibid 88.

154 Ibid 10.

155 Jacques Derrida, 'Force of Law: The "Mystical Foundation of Authority"', tr Mary Quaintance (1990) 11(5–6) *Cardozo Law Review* 920, 947.

156 Honig (n 152) 68.

5 Narratives of fire and apocalypse

Nicole Rogers

In previous chapters, I have explored the ways in which the megafires, in conjunction with other extraordinary phenomena in 2020, influenced the development of certain narratives in the public domain. The megafires are also playing a role in the evolution of fictitious narratives. Conversely, fictitious narratives have influenced our framing and interpretation of the megafires. In this final chapter, I consider fictitious narratives of fire and apocalypse, and the interplay of such narratives with the lived experience of the megafires.

Texts from the developing genre of Australian fire fiction increase awareness of the impacts of catastrophic fire events. Texts from broader categories of climate and apocalyptic fiction shape the ways in which we comprehend and adapt to such events. Drawing upon such works, I identify themes that resonate with, and provide insights into, our responses to the megafires and other climate disasters.

Fire fiction

Fire fiction, which focuses upon bushfires and their devastating impacts, is an established part of the Australian literary tradition dating back to the nineteenth century.[1] Notable twentieth century fire fiction encompasses a range of texts and can merge with official documentation; Kate Rigby describes the 1939 report of the Stretton Royal Commission,[2] with its powerful opening paragraphs, as 'a great work of Australian environmental literature'.[3] The report featured as a prescribed text in matriculation English in Victorian schools for many years.[4]

In her analysis of fire narratives, Rigby singles out Colin Thiele's *February Dragon*,[5] written as a 'cautionary tale'[6] for children at the behest of the South Australian Bush Fire Research Centre.[7] The message is clear, conveyed by a character in the opening chapters: it is generally human carelessness that causes fires.[8] This is later borne out when his sister-in-law's

DOI: 10.4324/b22677-5

failure to heed fire protocols unleashes the 'February dragon', a devastating fire which destroys the family property, pets and livestock, and endangers his family and much of the township. The dragon is finally 'driven back to his cage' by heavy rain, but there he '[waits] for another chance'.[9]

Ivan Southall's *Ash Road*[10] is another classic Australian children's book, published in the same year. Southall's descriptions of 'the world melting', of 'fire in the clouds hundreds of feet above the earth',[11] of 'waves of flame, torrents of flame'[12] from which there was 'no time to turn, no chance to turn, no place to turn',[13] highlight the magnitude and unstoppable ferocity of mid-twentieth century bushfires; these predated the rise in global temperatures but were, nevertheless, as Stephen Pyne puts it, 'fires of regime change'.[14] Southall's primary focus is upon the resilience of children, who must contend with a catastrophic fire event accidentally ignited by three teenage boys on a camping trip.

The climate-charged fires of the twenty-first century are reconfiguring the literary subset of fire fiction in the same way that they are transforming our natural and urban landscapes. Personal experience of a Tasmanian bushfire[15] underlies Amanda Lohrey's 2008 novella *Vertigo*, in which a couple abandon their house and shelter, with their neighbours, waist-deep in the 'slimy mud' of a nearby lagoon;[16] this particular scene evokes the terrifying experience of the many who immersed themselves in Lake Conjola on New Year's Eve in 2019, as a firestorm bore down on them.[17] Another work of climate fiction that appears to anticipate the megafires is Alice Robinson's 2015 novel *Anchor Point*,[18] in which Melbourne is ringed by huge fires, 'mired in smoke'[19] and left without power in a then futuristic, final scene: '[i]t was hard to believe that when it was over, there would be anything left to save'.[20]

The 2009 Victorian Black Saturday fires have inspired a powerful work of fire fiction from Alice Bishop, who lost her family home in the Christmas Hills at that time. In Bishop's collection of vignettes, some of which are only a paragraph in length, she documents the experiences of survivors and the broader community after the fires. A nameless narrator finds himself following the ghost of Elle, as she drives to and from her destroyed family home in her 'melted '99 Barina';[21] a nurse tries to forget the sufferings, 'the pain levels beyond imagination',[22] of burns victims. Bishop conveys a lingering, all-pervasive sense of loss and impermanence, as she writes from the viewpoint of the displaced and the bereaved. She conjures up colours and unforgettable images: 'betadine-and-copper-coloured smoke' and the remains of 'our neighbours', their 'amalgam fillings and tyre rims', in 'silvers, gunmetals and blacks'.[23] In the final story, Bishop shares her own memories. Prior to the fires, 'we sleep quietly in this unburnt house, still untouched by the disasters, natural and otherwise, we've seen on the news'.[24] In their aftermath, '[w]e know, now, that things can go'.[25]

In Eliza Henry Jones's *Ache*,[26] published in 2017, this new awareness of vulnerability and transience is processed by bushfire survivors: veterinarian Annie, who was persuaded by her grandmother to flee on horseback with her small daughter; her mother Susan, whose eccentricities have been exacerbated by the partial destruction of the family home and her mother's death; Annie's former boyfriend Alex, now a pariah after inadvertently igniting the inferno; and other members of a rural community trying to rally after the loss of family, properties and the surrounding forest. The author, a trauma counsellor, argues that fire fiction enables readers to 'explore the emotional and psychological impact of bushfires', and to recognise the broad spectrum of possible responses.[27]

The Angry Summer of 2012–2013 provides the context and temporal setting for Madeleine Watts's *The Inland Sea*.[28] As already flagged in Chapter 2, Watts is preoccupied with the 'splendid conflagration of emergency'[29] and its intrusion into the everyday. Fires burn uncontrollably throughout this novel: in the narrator's present; in her most traumatic childhood memories;[30] and in her futuristic vision of a derelict, abandoned Sydney.[31] They manifest in 'air glowing amber and thick',[32] in a 'blood-red sun and the orange glow of the skies'[33] and 'great clouds of flame'.[34] They threaten the desperate callers who ring for emergency assistance,[35] and leave ravaged landscapes in their wake.[36] The novel was published in March 2020, after Black Summer had officially ended. In April, another important work of Australian climate fiction appeared: James Bradley's *Ghost Species*.[37] The final editing of Bradley's book occurred during Black Summer[38] and, indeed, fires are a constant presence in this work as well.[39]

Writers of fiction did not hesitate to contribute commentary during and after Black Summer; some of this is featured in Sophie Cunningham's edited 2020 collection, *Fire, Flood and Plague*.[40] Other pieces appeared in media outlets.[41] Fictitious portrayals of Black Summer remain, however, very much an ongoing and future challenge for Australian writers.

Black Summer in fiction

In the Australian winter of 2020, Lucy Treloar, who set her 2019 climate fiction novel *Wolfe Island*[42] on a fictitious, inundated island in Chesapeake Bay rather than in drought-prone, fire-ravaged Australia, ruminated over the ways in which Black Summer would, or should, influence the writing of fiction in Australia. In a piece published in the literary magazine *Meanjin*, she wrote:

> It seemed like there were a thousand threads running through the season, stitching it all together, or fraying loose. A small insistent one for

> me was wondering how novelists will write in its aftermath. If we write about it, which things will we choose to leave out, and in what vein we will write them: as comedy, as tragedy, as portent, or as bit parts in the larger body of work? If we leave its effects entirely out of our next books, why? And will that absence be eloquent in a different way?[43]

Her conclusion was that novelists should try to stitch together the enormity of the megafires and climate change itself, with the themes of realist fiction. Perhaps, she wrote, 'the doors of realist fiction could be prised open enough just to indicate that characters have noticed that the world is changing'. The importance of this endeavour was underlined by Amitav Ghosh in 2016 when he identified the widespread 'patterns of evasion' and 'modes of concealment' in art and literature, the 'banishment' of climate change 'from the preserves of serious fiction'. He accused our cultural custodians of failing to alert people to the 'realities of their plight'.[44]

Richard Flanagan rises to this challenge in the first Australian offering of adult fire fiction after Black Summer: his 2020 novel *The Living Sea of Waking Dreams*.[45] Anticipating the conflagration, Flanagan wrote the initial draft in 2019, and then incorporated unsettling descriptions of Black Summer in the final version. He has stated that he 'wanted the novel invested with the urgency, the fear, the collapsing sense of time and possibility that such apocalyptic events create'.[46] Flanagan resorts to magical realism to convey his theme of vanishings and extinctions in the Anthropocene; characters inexplicably lose body parts throughout the novel. The devastating images of Black Summer are, however, very real: 'firefighters inside a fire truck swallowed by fire';[47] '[i]ncinerated kangaroos in foetal clutches of fencing wire charred koalas burnt bloated cattle on their backs';[48] 'a fire-created darkness at midday'.[49] This was '[a] world burning and nothing bringing it back'.[50]

Other books have been written for children and, in one instance, by children. One of the first pieces of Australian fiction to emerge in the aftermath of the megafires, and to directly address the subject matter of the fires, was a picture book by acclaimed children's author Jackie French. *Fire Wombat* was published at the end of 2020. The book is based on an injured wombat that staggered out of the bush, 'blackened by ash and charcoal': one of hundreds of animals to seek refuge at the author's Araluen home during the fires. When French was writing the book, her community was still traumatised, with children refusing to speak and adults stockpiling food and building bunkers. She has described writing as both a mechanism for 'processing a challenging year' and a 'form of "future proofing"', by 'build[ing] a child's imagination so that they can think creatively to prevent bushfires and pandemics'.[51]

Another book was produced by children from Cobargo Public School.[52] *The Day She Stole The Sun* was published in 2020 by Littlescribe, a writing platform of schools. Two of the children had lost family members and two had lost homes. The book provided a therapeutic outlet for children, who began to express emotions they had hitherto concealed.[53]

Australian fire fiction provides us with confronting insights into the experiences and emotions of victims and survivors. It can be didactic, as was the case with *February Dragon*. It can also, as discussed earlier, be therapeutic: a way of charting and stimulating the emotional recovery of survivors and communities in the aftermath of major fire events. There are overlaps between fire fiction and climate fiction. Furthermore, fire fiction, as exemplified in Flanagan's recent work, is increasingly taking on apocalyptic dimensions.

I turn now to considering the impact of speculative, or futuristic, climate and apocalyptic fiction in shaping responses to the megafires, and in reflecting the concerns and fears articulated during the megafires.

Apocalypse now

Sarah Walker and Fleur Kilpatrick argue that climate fiction set in the present lacks the compelling narrative structure of apocalyptic texts: 'the present tense is anticlimactic, problematic in its absence of drama'.[54] Yet, there was nothing anticlimactic about the megafires. As they took hold, impacted areas resembled the dystopias of climate and apocalyptic fiction in ways that were uncanny and disturbing. For this reason, owners of the bookshop in the destroyed township of Cobargo displayed a placard stating that '[p]ost-apocalyptic fiction [was] now moved to current affairs'.[55]

When the climate fiction television series *The Commons*[56] began screening on Christmas Day 2019, images depicting widespread social and environmental disruption in an imaginary near-future were juxtaposed, on Australian screens, with similar, real time images: of shocked, filthy climate refugees herded into evacuation centres, red and orange skies, heatwaves and encroaching fires. One reviewer suggested that 'our new bushfire reality' was 'moving faster than any production schedule'.[57]

Richard Flanagan, attempting to contextualise the megafires,[58] referenced two iconic, post-apocalyptic films with Australian settings: *Mad Max*[59] and *On the Beach*.[60] Another commentator found parallels with the orange skies which featured in the 2017 futuristic film *Blade Runner 2049*,[61] a vision in turn inspired by Sydney's red dust storms in 2009.[62] He was also reminded of the final scene in *Mad Max: Beyond Thunderdome*,[63] in which Sydney is depicted after a nuclear holocaust. For Kirsten Tranter, 'fragments of burnt forest' that appeared in Sydney streets conjured up the black flowers from a 1980s 'nuclear noir' television series.[64]

It could well be more than a semantic coincidence that the season of the megafires shares its name with a 2019 television series centred on a zombie apocalypse.[65] The words 'apocalypse' and 'apocalyptic' appeared frequently in media coverage and associated commentary on the Australian fires.[66] They surfaced in ordinary conversation[67] and in more formal settings, including a fundraising event in March at which Prince Charles described the fires 'as an apocalyptic vision of hell'.[68] The same metaphor was utilised later in 2020, as wildfires swept through the West Coast of the United States. The front page of the *Los Angeles Times* featured the heading 'California's Climate Apocalypse',[69] and Washington Governor Jay Inslee described the murky, smoke-filled vistas of his state as apocalyptic.[70]

The preceding examples of cross-referencing of apocalyptic and climate fiction texts, and the usage of apocalyptic language in commentary on the megafires, are indicative of our framing of ongoing encounters with the climate crisis and, as such, important: in Lisa Grow Sun's words, 'the way we narrate, describe, limit, and categorize disasters fundamentally shapes our approaches and solutions'.[71] The influence of apocalyptic and climate fiction texts on our understanding of the experience of Black Summer has bearing on our responses to the climate crisis, and on the ways in which we anticipate, prepare for and adapt to climate disaster.

Furthermore, as climate fiction novelist James Bradley puts it, 'the speculative futures of science fiction and allied genres provide a theatre for our anxieties and obsessions' and 'our imaginings of the end of the world reflect our own fears and concerns'.[72] In the next sections, I identify and discuss three prominent themes in contemporary climate and apocalyptic fiction; these themes align with particular fears and concerns that surfaced during Black Summer. Here, again, we are confronted with scalar difficulties in processing and addressing the climate crisis.

Apocalyptic parenting

The extent to which climate disasters imperil even children of the Global North became manifest during the megafires; consequently, parental anxiety about the survival and future wellbeing of their children was exacerbated. In apocalyptic and climate fiction texts, we can find numerous expressions of parental concern and depictions of parochial parenting practices. There is a correlation between the reactions of parents and would-be parents during the megafires, and the emphasis in speculative climate and apocalyptic fiction on saving one's own offspring.

Children were uniquely vulnerable during the megafires.[73] The confronting image of 11-year-old Finn Burns, wearing a face mask and steering a small boat under a blood red sky as his family fled his hometown of Mallacoota, was one of many widely circulated on social, national and international media outlets;[74] it was, he said later, a 'really scary' moment. Mental health workers noted the rise in the number of young people presenting with anxiety and depression.[75] A child welfare expert stated to the Royal Commission on the second day of the hearings that disasters 'are no longer perceived as rare events; they are often seen as climate change and they're part of our new reality'. She pointed out that the loss of hope, and the realisation that parents cannot necessarily protect their children in this new reality, left children traumatised in the wake of the fires.[76]

Parents found themselves contending with unprecedented hazards and challenges as the fires impacted upon their families. One father wrote a public letter to the Prime Minister, stating that he could no longer support the Liberal Party given its staunch refusal to act on climate change; this decision was made as his 'family lay face-down in the sand, covered in wet blankets on Malua Bay Beach as hot embers rained down'.[77] He was not the only parent trying to comfort frightened children while the sky turned red and black, and fires raged through bushland towards them.[78] Others found themselves similarly trapped with their children on beaches and wharves, and in stationary cars and over-crowded evacuation centres.

Researchers, in surveying the 'eco-reproductive concerns' of American adults, have noted widespread 'concern, anxiety, and even anguish about the climate impacts that participants expected their existing, expected, or hypothetical children to experience in the course of their lifetimes'.[79] The megafires exacerbated these reactions. In Sydney and Canberra, the two capital cities most affected by bushfire smoke, parents worried about the exposure of their children to toxic air.[80] A Canberra obstetrician commented that 'every single parent-to-be tells me they are fearful for their child's climate future'.[81] Public health researcher Gemma Carey wrote that the experience of living through 'climate collapse' in smoke-filled Canberra 'changed us all'. She commented that 'if we choose to parent we will have to prepare our children to survive in a very different world while we ourselves try to understand how it is changing'.[82]

The central question of whether the decision to become a parent is wise or sensible, in light of deteriorating conditions for planetary health, is echoed in climate fiction. Eadie, a principal character in *The Commons*, articulates this quandary after witnessing the impact of a climate disaster on a bereaved mother: 'I'm struggling to remember why I thought having a baby, when it's like this, was a good idea'.[83] Parenting challenges in apocalyptic and post-apocalyptic scenarios are canvassed at length in contemporary climate fiction texts, with an accompanying emphasis on the tenacity of parent love. Our current preoccupations, and fears for our children, find expression in such texts.

In the 2020 climate fiction novel *The New Wilderness*, Bea, driven by her desperation to save her daughter's life, volunteers for a grand experiment in living as hunter-gatherers in the Wilderness State. The sacrifices required of her are immense: '*This is motherhood?* she thought, furious and broken-hearted as she tried to let go of her own self so she could free her arms to hold up Agnes'.[84] Agnes, in turn, eventually finds herself mothering a child, Fern, whom she has rescued: '[Fern] knows she has everything I can give her'.[85] Another example of parochial parenting appears in Lauren Beukes' *Afterland*, also a 2020 publication. Cole, attempting to save her son in the dysfunctional dystopia of a plague-ridden United States, expresses relief with the words 'Thank you, climate change', when the explanation for a police roadblock on the highway is forest fire rather than pursuit.[86] In climate fiction novels such as *The Mother Fault*[87] and *After the Flood*,[88] parents are prepared to risk the lives of others in order to protect their children. Such works suggest the necessity for single-minded focus and ruthlessness in apocalyptic parenting.

Parental anxiety about the climate crisis and related disasters is at the heart of Jenny Offill's novel *Weather*,[89] published in 2020 to widespread acclaim. It informs the narrator Lizzie's attempts to prepare for catastrophe as she parents, works, half-heartedly contemplates an affair, and looks after a vulnerable sibling. It underlies the destructive visions[90] of her brother, a recovering addict and new parent. The author has stated that she originally envisaged the book as a survival manual for her daughter.[91] Parenting concerns are also very much central to *Ghost Species*[92] and *Fauna*:[93] two other climate fiction texts released in 2020. In both, mothers face the novel challenge of raising genetically engineered, Neanderthal daughters. The task of protecting these unique children overshadows all other considerations, leading to broken relationships, the sacrifice of a career and even, in *Fauna*, the eventual loss of the mother's other children.[94]

Adeline Johns-Putra has alluded to the dangers in adopting 'parental care as an ethical position' in climate fiction, and more generally.[95] Intergenerational equity, and a safe climate for the world's children, can be achieved only through broad, global changes and societal transformation. Scalar issues are evident here, as parental zooming in on their own children, and overriding anxiety about their safety, obfuscate this important point. Johns-Putra argues, however, that, the climate change novel can redress this by providing 'a response from the one "cared-for"':[96] the children themselves. In *Afterland*, for instance, Cole's son 'tenses up' at his mother's relief at the burning of 'the whole forest', 'the lungs of the world'; she belatedly '[tries] to correct herself'.[97] Similarly, participants in the school strike movement, while drawing upon survivalist rhetoric, refuse to engage in 'the power games and conflicts that potentially mark and mar parental care ethics'.[98] During Black Summer, despite the health risks created by toxic air, Australian children continued to assemble in large, outdoor gatherings. There they spoke out boldly about the need for climate action. Their planetary-scaled concerns transcended their own immediate wellbeing.

No safe place

Black Summer made clear the impermanence and precarity of a climate-disrupted future. Refuges were ephemeral and illusory. Sheltering in place did not offer any form of safety; this reinforced the painful lesson from the Black Saturday fires in 2009, when more than half of the fatalities occurred inside people's houses.[99] As the former governor of the Bank of England pointed out during the pandemic, 'we can't self-isolate' from climate change.[100]

Bronwyn Adcock, after experiencing the Currowan fire on the south coast of New South Wales, has written that '[i]t would give us a day where there was no safe place left to be'.[101] A long-term Coonabarabran resident, who was twice evacuated during Black Summer, contemplated leaving her hometown but wondered where to find 'a safer place when so much of the nation was burning in so many places you'd never expect'.[102] Author Sophie Cunningham wrote that her 'imagined safe havens' for end times 'had been burnt beyond recognition', and remarked: 'What a delusion it was that we – that any of us – could dodge what was coming'.[103] Novelist Jane Rawson was similarly aghast when, two days after her relocation to Tasmania, bushfires threatened the new home that she had wrongly assumed would provide a climate refuge.[104] Caught up in an 'endless cycle'[105] of bushfire risk and repeated emergency warnings in the Tasmanian fires of 2019, she described the experience as 'a metaphor of our future under climate change': 'at any point it could be you getting the emergency warning, you who has to flee, but only if the path is clear'.[106]

This revelation from Black Summer is consistent with scientific predictions. One scientist undertaking research on the accelerated rate of warming in Antarctica[107] has pointed out that 'there's no place on earth that's immune to global warming', and concluded that '[t]here's nowhere to hide – not even up on the Antarctic Plateau'.[108] Nevertheless, growing numbers of people are attempting to create potential refuges for end times, as Mark O'Connell and Bradley Garrett have documented in two provocative works of non-fiction released in 2020: *Notes from an Apocalypse*[109] and *Bunker*.[110] Novelist Lauren Graff, who has also researched the burgeoning phenomenon of survivalism in the United States, admits that she herself has prepared a climate refuge for her family.[111]

The survivalist mentality, with its accompanying 'lifeboat ethics' as propounded by Garrett Hardin,[112] has been described by psychotherapist Paul

Hoggett as 'a demoralised state of mind in which questions of value have been progressively destroyed'.[113] By propelling us forward in time, past the point of no return and into the looming climate apocalypse, futuristic climate fiction might be seen to encourage such a mentality with all its moral deficits. This is particularly the case with climate fiction that presupposes the existence of climate refugia:[114] a term commonly used within the discipline of environmental sciences to signify a place where ecosystems and species can flourish despite climate disruptions, but one which could also encompass climate havens for certain privileged humans. There is a disjunction between the realisation that there is no safe place, and portrayals of climate refugia as offering permanence in an impermanent world, stability and safety in increasingly precarious times. Examples of such fictitious refugia abound.

In Julie Bertagna's *Exodus* trilogy,[115] the interior of Greenland becomes a sanctuary for climate refugees displaced by extensive sea level rise. The privileged minority reside in elevated sky cities. In the film *Waterworld*,[116] again featuring a largely inundated planet, the directions to a climate refugia can be found in a tattoo on the back of a young girl; final scenes depict an unspoilt coastline with waterfalls, forests and beaches. In Sally Abbott's *Closing Down*,[117] the House of Many Promises, constructed over constantly replenishing springs, provides an implausible sanctuary from fire that threatens to engulf a rural township. In *Cargo*,[118] a post-apocalyptic Australian film, Aboriginal characters escape a deadly pandemic by relocating to Wilpena Pound: a green, forested valley in the midst of the South Australian desert. The island of Tasmania represents security and safety in *The Glad Shout*,[119] although it has become largely inaccessible and its borders are heavily guarded. It also provides refuge from an uninhabitable Australian mainland in *The Warming*,[120] and is the destination for indentured climate refugees, 'dumped . . . as citizens of nowhere', in Rohan Wilson's *Daughter of Bad Times*.[121] In light of its 'relative isolation and potential resilience in an unstable world',[122] billionaire Davis Hucken selects the island as the location for his Foundation, and his ambitious, genetic experiments in reversing extinction, in *Ghost Species*. In popular mythology, Tasmania vies with New Zealand, the 'ark of nation-states',[123] as climate haven.

Other texts adopt a more sceptical approach to the concept of climate refugia. Lizzie, in *Weather*, 'can't seem to escape that question' of '[w]hat will be the safest place'.[124] She recognises, nevertheless, that this approach is contrary to the televised advice of a climatologist,[125] and her somewhat impractical preparations, the collection of bizarre and practical survival tips, listing the necessary characteristics of a 'doomstead',[126] are counterbalanced with her wry, compassionate insights into her everyday encounters and exchanges. In the television series *The Commons*, Dom, whose insider status provides him with first-hand knowledge of looming calamities, purchases a rural property from a desperate family. He describes it as a 'bolthole'[127] and recites to his family the features that render it, in his view, the ideal refugia: its inaccessibility other than by air; the pristine, permanent watercourse; and the surrounding national park.[128] The river is, however, full of contaminants[129] and, for viewers simultaneously watching the terrifying images of the Black Summer megafires, the forested valley represents a firetrap.

The ephemeral nature of climate refuges is also highlighted in a number of fictitious texts. In Alexis Wright's formidable, futuristic *The Swan Book*,[130] the swamp, to which Aboriginal traditional owners from all around Australia have been forcibly relocated,[131] becomes the home of European climate refugee Bella Donna.[132] Even this dubious refuge, a stagnant 'dumping ground' for unwanted people[133] and 'rotten and broken-down vessels',[134] is eventually destroyed by the Army.[135] In *A Children's Bible*,[136] in the wake of a climate disaster, a group of children find their rural retreat invaded by opportunistic and violent scavengers;[137] they create a more fortified and urban version[138] but its longevity is uncertain. In *Ghost Species*, Tasmania experiences climatic disturbances and societal breakdown, and hidden, self-sufficient, rural communities are raided.[139] In this text[140] and others, including *The New Wilderness*, *Station Eleven*[141] and *The Road*,[142] a reversion to the hunter-gatherer lifestyle decentres the myth of refuges. Such portrayals are underpinned by a different but still problematic set of assumptions about end times, and the route by which humanity has travelled there. Claire Colebrook has pointed out that '[t]he forms of life that capitalism, imperialism, colonisation and slavery already extinguished – indigenous and nomadic – are the very forms that are deployed to depict the end of the world, but always in a perverse and fantasmic form'.[143]

The seductiveness of climate refugia as a concept is symptomatic of the scalar complexities in comprehending and addressing the hyperobject of climate change. Individuals feel powerless to prevent the steep rise in global emissions and the rapid warming of the planet; their focus, then, shifts to protecting themselves and their families. This parochial focus is consistent with the Australian government's endorsement of adaptation and resilience in preference to mitigation, increasingly an isolationist stance.[144] The megafires made a mockery of such attempts at self-preservation. In Danielle Celermajer's words, we saw that the 'walls that held us safe' are 'made of dominoes, and they are falling'.[145] There is 'no protective shield',[146] no safe place.

The new normal and Anthropocene disorder

Black Summer provided a disturbing preview of Australia's future. We no longer needed climate fiction writers, or scientific modelling, to open portals for us into the climate apocalypse; we had been catapulted into it, and we were seemingly powerless to alter it. During Black Summer, Australians spoke and wrote about a 'new normal'. For one survivor, this state encompassed 'summers spent indoors lest the air chokes us all, Christmas under slate and noxious skies, evacuation orders covering ever-larger concentric circles until, at last, there is nothing left to burn and nowhere left to run'.[147] References to a 'new normal' subsequently took on a different character throughout the pandemic-related disruptions of 2020.

Climate fiction writers are adept at portraying a 'new normal'. In part, this arises from the futuristic nature of most climate fiction. Characters adjust, and must adjust, in futuristic settings, to compromised air quality that causes lethal disease,[148] polluted oceans and living within protective domes,[149] acid rain and destructive cyclones,[150] flooding and sea level rise.[151] Similarly, Australians adjusted to the 'everyday nature of catastrophe' during Black Summer.[152] David Wallace-Wells, author of a 2019 non-fiction work called *An Uninhabitable Earth*,[153] observed at the time that Australia appeared uninhabitable from a distance; nevertheless, he surmised, Australians would continue living there, adapting to hitherto unimaginable conditions. He reflected that the most likely global scenario in coming decades was

> not the extinction of the human race nor the total collapse of civilization, but dystopias all the more terrifying for seeming "normal" to those living in them, however horrific they may seem from the distance of a decade or a few thousand miles.[154]

There is, however, inherent danger in any acceptance of a new normal at this critical juncture in planetary history. Geographer Lesley Head wrote, in the aftermath of the fires, that climate denialists tend to present 'the new normal' as 'a set of new stable conditions that we can get used to'; this downplays or ignores the reality of 'accelerating change'.[155] James Bradley similarly pointed out during Black Summer that this was not the new normal but, rather, 'just the beginning'.[156] Jennifer Mills speculated that '[w]e use this kind of language because accepting a "new normal" is easier than accepting that the window of hospitality that life on earth has enjoyed thus far is being closed'. She argues that writers have an obligation 'to integrate [climate disasters] into our understanding of the reality we live in' but, also, that they 'must refuse to accept them as normal'.[157] The 'new normal' represents a kind of blindness.[158]

The growing recourse to the phrase 'the new normal' can be viewed as an adaptive mechanism in the face of what Timothy Clark designates Anthropocene disorder: 'the intellectual, moral and political insecurity that accompanies the derangement of given norms'.[159] Clark argues that the difficulties inherent in connecting everyday experiences with their scale effects, or comprehending the magnitude of 'slow-motion catastrophe' and the consequential paucity of current mitigatory measures, add up to 'a new kind of psychic disorder'.[160] There is, here, a realised sense of multiple realities as a consequence of the different, scalar framings of the Anthropocene: the reality of our embodied existence in the everyday world, in which our actions have discernible impact on our surroundings and physical beings, and the planetary reality that is climate change, in which the global aggregate of those actions forces large-scale changes to our physical environment but the impact of our individual actions is miniscule.

During Black Summer, the magnitude of the megafires, and a corresponding sense of individual powerlessness, exacerbated the uneasiness, dislocation and loss of certainty associated with Anthropocene disorder. In one powerful piece, writer Mark Mordue wrote about the 'profound feeling of futility and depression' that descended upon him as he, and his fellow Sydney residents, 'slowly smothered' in the toxic air of Black Summer.[161]

Depictions of Anthropocene disorder also appear in climate fiction and, indeed, in apocalyptic fiction. Eleanor Smith, analysing two apocalyptic texts,[162] has observed that '[t]hemes of denial and helplessness run through each text as the characters struggle to reconcile their intimate, personal worlds with a global one in ruins'.[163] In a sense, all climate fiction displays the scalar incongruities underlying the condition of Anthropocene disorder. Clark has highlighted the disjuncture between the literary techniques commonly deployed to 'engage a reader's immediate emotional interest', and 'the scale, complexity and the multiple and nonhuman contexts' of the Anthropocene.[164] The climate crisis itself '[juxtaposes] the trivial and the catastrophic in ways that can be deranging or paralyzing'.[165] Two 2020 climate fiction texts that address this uneasy juxtaposition and its paralysing effects are *The Living Sea of the Waking Dead* and *Weather*.[166]

Flanagan captures the allure of the artificial world of social media, the temptation to sink into the world of '[l]ike share update friend subscribe'.[167] Anna, a central character, flicks through its endless images, the 'meaningless droplets briefly lit before going dark', in order to avoid thinking about the unfolding planetary catastrophe,[168] her mother's protracted dying[169] and the inexplicable disappearance of body parts. Given that 'real lives' are contained within 'the smallness of [people's] phones',[170] it is unsurprising that such vanishings are neither acknowledged nor addressed by those around her. Grief and loss, even despair, can be sublimated into a wave of Instagram posts. Yet, Instagram, that 'blessed Novocaine of the soul',[171] also transports her into the horror of Black Summer: 'Anna couldn't bear to read it she couldn't bear to think'.[172] Images of dead wildlife and 'medieval tableaux of muted humanity on beaches in the ochre wash of an inferno' are intermingled with '[s]hoes dresses kitchenware'.[173]

In *Weather*, Lizzie's awareness of the imminence of the climate crisis sits oddly with her everyday existence as mother, wife, sister and urban dweller: this is the very essence of Anthropocene disorder. As one reviewer has written, Offill is documenting 'the daily experience of scale-shifting', as Lizzie moves 'between the claustrophobia of domestic discontent and the impossibly vast horizon of global catastrophe'.[174] The very structure of the text, with its fragmented anecdotes, conveys the scalar deformities inherent in the lifestyles of privileged citizens of the Global North. Lizzie is rendered as immobilised as Anna by what Amitav Ghosh has described as 'the inertia of habitual motion'.[175]

Conclusion

These final reflections upon the new normal, and Anthropocene disorder, have a broader significance beyond narratives of fiction and can be related back to the narratives canvassed in earlier chapters. The account of developing narratives of emergency throughout 2020, in Chapter 2, demonstrates the ongoing seepage of emergency into everyday life that is a feature of the new normal. A focus upon immediate emergency and the construction of a hierarchy of emergency at any given time have the same origins as Anthropocene disorder: in the deep-rooted resistance to multiple scalar framings and doubled realities.

The various narratives of culpability discussed in Chapter 3 illustrate the need to find explanations, and assign blame, for climate disasters such as the megafires. Through these efforts, the new normal is assimilated within established frameworks and institutions, including legal apparatuses. Yet it is difficult to reconcile such narratives, and legal narratives in particular, with the global scale of the climate crisis. In this respect, narratives of culpability can compound Anthropocene disorder.

Finally, narratives of protest, and their manifestation in courtrooms, are very much driven by Anthropocene disorder. Climate activists refuse to accept climate disasters as the new normal. In striving for climate justice, read broadly to incorporate social justice outcomes, they seek transformative change on multiple levels, and in multiple frames.

As this journey through the public narratives of 2020, and their fictitious counterparts, has revealed, the megafires and the pandemic transformed our understanding of emergency and its particular temporalities. Both phenomena required us to re-evaluate existing assumptions about public and personal safety. The fires prompted young people and mainstream Australians to engage in protest activities, and led to a range of different lawsuits. They influenced emerging narratives of climate fiction and resonated with existing themes in fictitious narratives. They precipitated an urgent debate on the ways in which the climate emergency should be addressed, a debate to some extent suspended by the competing imperative of resolving a global health crisis.

Trapped within the flames and smoke of the megafires, Australians adapted but, simultaneously, experienced the unsettling awareness of the disjuncture between our current lifestyles and planetary changes. The onset of the pandemic diluted such concerns and added a different and arguably overriding dimension to the emergency narratives at play. Nevertheless, in public fora and in fiction, the fires left an indelible mark throughout 2020 and beyond, shaping official, legal and activist narratives and reminding us that adaptation alone cannot shield us from future climate disasters of equal or greater magnitude.

Notes

1 See Grace Moore, 'Fires, Literature, Politics and Mateship in the Bush' (2013) 48(4) *Agora* 53.
2 *Royal Commission into the Causes of, and Measures Taken to Prevent the Bush Fires of January, 1939, and to Protect Life and Property, and the Measures to be Taken to Prevent Bush Fires in Victoria and to Protect Life and Property in the Event of Future Bush Fires* (Final Report, 16 May 1939).
3 Kate Rigby, *Dancing with Disaster: Environmental Histories, Narratives and Ethics for Perilous Times* (University of Virginia Press, 2015) 125.
4 Ibid 128.
5 Colin Thiele, *February Dragon* (Weldon, 1966).
6 Rigby (n 3) 128.
7 Ibid 129.
8 Thiele (n 5) 23.
9 Ibid 174.
10 Ivan Southall, *Ash Road* (Puffin Books, 1966).
11 Ibid 167.
12 Ibid 131–2.
13 Ibid 132.
14 Stephen Pyne, *The Still-Burning Bush* (Scribe, rev ed, 2020) 41.
15 Jane Sullivan, 'The Fire of Fiction', *The Age* (online, 15 November 2008) <www.theage.com.au/entertainment/books/the-fire-of-fiction-20081115-ge7ink.html>.
16 Amanda Lohrey, *Vertigo* (Black Inc, ebook, 2009) 57.
17 Sean Rubinsztein-Dunlop and John Stewart, 'The Water Stopped: But the Fire Kept Coming', *ABC News* (online, 8 June 2020) <www.abc.net.au/news/2020-06-08/witness-accounts-of-new-years-eve-bushfire-at-conjola/12317258?nw=0>.
18 Alice Robinson, *Anchor Point* (Affirm Press, 2015).
19 Ibid 254.
20 Ibid 258.
21 Alice Bishop, *A Constant Hum* (Text Publishing, 2019) 60.
22 Ibid 86.

23 Ibid 119.
24 Ibid 195.
25 Ibid 197.
26 Eliza Henry Jones, *Ache* (Fourth Estate, 2017)
27 Eliza Henry Jones, 'Bushfires Shape Australia's Landscape: But the Trauma Burns On and On', *The Guardian* (online, 22 May 2017) <www.theguardian.com/books/2017/may/22/bushfires-shape-australias-landscape-but-the-trauma-burns-on-and-on>.
28 Madeleine Watts, *The Inland Sea* (ONE, 2020).
29 Ibid 68.
30 Ibid 132.
31 Ibid 245–6.
32 Ibid 47.
33 Ibid 119.
34 Ibid 228.
35 Ibid 40–1, 225–7.
36 Ibid 82.
37 James Bradley, *Ghost Species* (Hamish Hamilton, 2020).
38 James Bradley, 'Could Bringing Neanderthals Back to Life Save the Environment? The Idea Is Not Quite Science Fiction', *The Guardian* (online, 27 April 2020) <www.theguardian.com/books/2020/apr/27/could-bringing-neanderthals-back-to-life-save-the-environment-the-idea-is-not-quite-science-fiction>.
39 Bradley (n 37) 81, 168, 196, 201, 213, 225, 265.
40 Sophie Cunningham (ed), *Fire, Flood, Plague: Australian Writers Respond to 2020* (Vintage Books, 2020).
41 See, eg, novelist Charlotte Wood's article 'From Disbelief to Dread: The Dismal New Routine of Life in Sydney's Smoke Haze', *The Guardian* (online, 7 December 2019) <www.theguardian.com/australia-news/2019/dec/07/from-disbelief-to-dread-the-dismal-new-routine-of-life-in-sydneys-smoke-haze>.
42 Lucy Treloar, *Wolfe Island* (Pan Macmillan Australia, 2019).
43 Lucy Treloar, 'Writing the Apocalypse' (Winter 2020) *Meanjin* <https://meanjin.com.au/essays/writing-the-apocalypse>.
44 Amitav Ghosh, *The Great Derangement: Climate Change and the Unthinkable* (University of Chicago Press, 2016) 11.
45 Richard Flanagan, *The Living Sea of Waking Dreams* (Knopf, 2020).
46 'Richard Flanagan on His Astonishing New Novel, The Living Sea of Waking Dreams', *Better Reading* (Blog Post, 18 October 2020) <www.betterreading.com.au/review/richard-flanagan-on-his-astonishing-new-novel-the-living-sea-of-waking-dreams>.
47 Flanagan (n 45) 98.
48 Ibid 100.
49 Ibid.
50 Ibid 98.
51 Melanie Kembrey, 'Children's Author Jackie French and the Little Wombat That Could', *The Sydney Morning Herald* (online, 4 July 2020) <www.smh.com.au/culture/books/children-s-author-jackie-french-and-the-little-wombat-that-could-20200703-p558ww.html>.
52 Cobargo was one of the worst affected communities during Black Summer, with many properties and two lives lost.

53 Jordan Baker, 'Tale of Loss and Hope: The Children Helping Fire-Ravaged Cobargo Heal', *The Sydney Morning Herald* (online, 13 November 2020) <www.smh.com.au/education/tale-of-loss-and-hope-the-children-helping-fire-ravaged-cobargo-heal-20201113-p56ebv.html>.
54 Sarah Walker and Fleur Kilpatrick, 'Sinking Feelings and Hopeful Horizons: Holding Complexity in Climate Change Theatre' in Anne M Harris and Stacy Holman Jones (eds), *Affective Movements, Methods and Pedagogies* (Routledge, 2020) 83, 87.
55 Baz Ruddick, 'Building Community in a Scorched Summer' in Michael Rowland (ed), *Black Summer* (Harper Collins, 2021) 251, 261.
56 *The Commons* (Playmaker, 2019).
57 Craig Mathieson, 'The Commons Predicted Climate Apocalypse: Then an Actual One Happened', *The Sydney Morning Herald* (online, 7 January 2020) <www.smh.com.au/culture/tv-and-radio/the-commons-predicted-climate-apocalypse-then-an-actual-one-happened-20200106-p53pax.html>.
58 Richard Flanagan, 'Australia Is Committing Climate Suicide', *The New York Times* (online, 3 January 2020) <www.nytimes.com/2020/01/03/opinion/australia-fires-climate-change.html>.
59 *Mad Max* (Byron Kennedy, 1979).
60 *On the Beach* (Lomitas Productions, 1959).
61 *Blade Runner 2049* (Columbia Pictures, 2017).
62 Simon Caterson, 'City of Light, Air and Impending Doom', *The Australian* (online, 13 December 2019) <www.theaustralian.com.au/inquirer/sydneys-apocalyptic-history/news-story/1f36d849931e6e394e0c4842030520a2>.
63 *Mad Max: Beyond Thunderdome* (George Miller, 1985).
64 Kirsten Tranter, 'Black Flowers: Mourning in Ashes' in Cunningham (n 40) 19, 19.
65 *Black Summer* (The Asylum, 2019).
66 See, eg, Isabella Kwai, 'Apocalyptic Scenes in Australia as Fires Turn Skies Blood Red', *The New York Times* (online, 31 December 2019) <www.nytimes.com/2019/12/31/world/australia/fires-red-skies-Mallacoota.html>.
67 Treloar (n 43).
68 Latika Bourke, 'Australian Bushfires Like "Apocalyptic Vision of Hell", Says Prince Charles', *The Sydney Morning Herald* (online, 13 March 2020) <www.smh.com.au/world/europe/australian-bushfires-like-apocalyptic-vision-of-hell-says-prince-charles-20200313-p549qv.html>.
69 Susanne Rust and Tony Barboza, 'California's Climate Apocalypse', (13 September 2020) *Los Angeles Times* 1.
70 Allie Bice, 'Washington Gov. Inslee Says State Looks "Apocalyptic" From Fires', *Politico* (online, 13 September 2020) <www.politico.com/news/2020/09/13/inslee-wildfires-climate-change-413593>.
71 Lisa Grow Sun, 'Climate Change and the Narrative of Disaster' in Jacqueline Peel and David Fisher (eds), *The Role of International Environmental Law in Disaster Risk Reduction* (Brill, 2016) 29, 29.
72 James Bradley, 'The Library at the End of the World' (13 October 2020) *Sydney Review of Books* <https://sydneyreviewofbooks.com/essay/library-end-world-bradley>.
73 Colin Brinsden, 'Children's Needs Overlooked in Bushfires', *The Canberra Times* (online, 25 April 2020) <www.canberratimes.com.au/story/6735099/childrens-needs-overlooked-in-bushfires>.

74 Ashleigh McMillan and Anthony Colangelo, '"Just Worried about Getting Away from the Fire": Mallacoota's Boat Boy Speaks Out', *The Age* (online, 1 January 2020) <www.theage.com.au/national/victoria/just-worried-about-getting-away-from-the-fire-mallacoota-s-boat-boy-speaks-out-20200101-p53o5n.html>.

75 Nick O'Malley and Peter Hannam, 'The New Dread of Australia's Once-Loved Long, Hot Summer', *The Sydney Morning Herald* (online, 29 February 2020) <www.smh.com.au/national/nsw/the-new-dread-of-australia-s-once-loved-long-hot-summer-20200228-p545di.html>.

76 Nick O'Malley, 'Bushfires Left Estimated 445 Dead From Smoke and a Nation Traumatised', *The Sydney Morning Herald* (online, 26 May 2020) <www.smh.com.au/environment/climate-change/bushfires-left-estimated-445-dead-from-smoke-and-a-nation-traumatised-20200526-p54wha.html>.

77 Angus McFarlane, 'I've Always Voted Liberal, But after Sheltering My Family on a Beach I Cannot Support This Government', *The Guardian* (online, 3 January 2020) <theguardian.com/commentisfree/2020/jan/03/ive-always-voted-liberal-but-after-sheltering-my-family-on-a-beach-i-cannot-support-this-government>.

78 Stephen Lunn, 'Bushfires Disaster: Thousands Stranded in New Year's Eve Fury', *The Australian* (online, 31 December 2019) <www.theaustralian.com.au/nation/bushfires-crisis-thousands-stranded-in-new-years-eve-fury/news-story/b65fc8b80c92fa31c79cfbd91c12aa44>.

79 Matthew Schneider-Mayerson and Kit Ling Leong, 'Eco-Reproductive Concerns in the Age of Climate Change' (2020) 163 *Climatic Change* 1007, 1015.

80 Venetia Vecellio, '"I've Cried, Apologising to My Baby for Bringing Him into This"', *The Sydney Morning Herald* (online, 10 January 2020) <www.smh.com.au/lifestyle/health-and-wellness/i-ve-cried-apologising-to-my-baby-for-bringing-him-into-this-20200109-p53q6v.html> .

81 Amy Remeikis, 'Canberra Chokes on World's Worst Air Quality as City All But Shut Down', *The Guardian* (online, 3 January 2020) <www.theguardian.com/australia-news/2020/jan/03/canberra-chokes-on-worlds-worst-air-quality-as-city-all-but-shut-down>.

82 Gemma Carey, 'Being Pregnant in a Climate Emergency Was an Existential Challenge: Miscarriage Has Brought a New Grief', *The Guardian* (online, 10 January 2020) <www.theguardian.com/commentisfree/2020/jan/10/being-pregnant-in-a-climate-emergency-was-an-existential-challenge-miscarriage-has-brought-a-new-grief>.

83 'Season 1, Episode 4', *The Commons* (n 56) 0:35:01–0:35:06.

84 Diane Cook, *The New Wilderness* (Harper, 2020) 73.

85 Ibid 394.

86 Lauren Beukes, *Afterland* (Michael Joseph, 2020) 293.

87 Kate Mildenhall, *The Mother Fault* (Simon and Schuster, 2020).

88 Kassandra Montag, *After the Flood* (Harper Collins, 2019).

89 Jenny Offill, *Weather* (Granta, 2020).

90 Ibid 176.

91 Parul Sehgal, 'How to Write Fiction When the Planet Is Falling Apart' (5 February 2020) *The New York Times Magazine* <www.nytimes.com/2020/02/05/magazine/jenny-offill-weather-book.html>.

92 Bradley (n 37).

93 Donna Mazza, *Fauna* (Allen and Unwin, 2020).
94 Ibid 307.
95 Adeline Johns-Putra, *Climate Change and the Contemporary Novel* (Cambridge University Press, 2019) 56.
96 Ibid 57.
97 Beukes (n 86) 293.
98 Johns-Putra (n 95) 57.
99 See Joshua Whittaker et al, 'Experiences of Sheltering during the Black Saturday Bushfires: Implications for Policy and Research' (2017) 23 *International Journal of Disaster Risk Reduction* 119.
100 Victoria Gill, 'Mark Carney: "We Can't Self-Isolate from Climate Change"', *BBC News* (online, 7 May 2020) <www.bbc.com/news/science-environment-52582243>.
101 Bronwyn Adcock, 'Living Hell' (February 2020) *The Monthly* <www.themonthly.com.au/issue/2020/february/1580475600/bronwyn-adcock/living-hell#mtr>.
102 Susan Harris Rimmer, 'Leaving Coonabarabran: Who Will Be Australia's Climate Refugees?' (2020) *Griffith Review* <www.griffithreview.com/articles/leaving-coonabarabran>.
103 Sophie Cunningham, 'If You Choose to Stay, We May Not Be Able to Save You' (Winter 2020) *Meanjin* <https://meanjin.com.au/essays/if-you-choose-to-stay-we-may-not-be-able-to-save-you>.
104 Jane Rawson, 'But How Are We Supposed to Have Any Fun?' in Cameron Muir, Kirsten Wehner and Jenny Newell (eds), *Living with the Anthropocene: Love, Loss and Hope in the Face of Environmental Crisis* (NewSouth, 2020) 41, 46–49.
105 Ibid 41, 48.
106 Ibid 49.
107 See Kyle R Clem et al, 'Record Warming at the South Pole during the Last Three Decades' (2020) 10 *Nature Climate Change* 762.
108 Quoted in Peter Hannam, '"Nowhere to Hide": South Pole Warms Up with Climate Change a Factor', *The Sydney Morning Herald* (online, 30 June 2020) <www.smh.com.au/environment/climate-change/nowhere-to-hide-south-pole-warms-up-with-climate-change-a-factor-20200629-p55797.html>.
109 Mark O'Connell, *Notes from an Apocalypse: A Personal Journey to the End of the World and Back* (Granta, 2020).
110 Bradley Garrett, *Bunker: Building for the End Times* (Allen Lane, 2020).
111 Lauren Groff, 'Waiting for the End of the World' (26 February 2020) *Harpers Magazine* <https://harpers.org/archive/2020/03/waiting-for-the-end-of-the-world-lauren-groff>.
112 See Paul Hoggett, 'Climate Change and the Apocalyptic Imagination' (2011) 16 *Psychoanalysis, Culture and Society* 261, 268–9. Garrett Hardin wrote about lifeboat ethics in 'Lifeboat Ethics: The Case against Helping the Poor' (1974) 8 *Psychology Today* 38.
113 Hoggett (n 112) 273.
114 Jo Chandler provides the following definition of climate refugia: 'A geographical region that has remained unaltered by a climatic change affecting surrounding regions and that therefore forms a haven for relict fauna and flora'; Jo Chandler, 'Weekend in Gondwana' in Muir, Wehner and Newell (n 104) 55, 55.

115 Julie Bertagna, *Exodus* (Picador, 2002); Julia Bertagna, *Zenith* (Picador, 2007); Julie Bertagna, *Aurora* (Macmillan, 2011).
116 *Waterworld* (Gordon Company, 1995).
117 Sally Abbott, *Closing Down* (Hachette, 2017).
118 *Cargo* (Umbrella Entertainment, 2017).
119 Alice Robinson, *The Glad Shout* (Affirm Press, 2019).
120 Craig Ensor, *The Warming* (Simon and Schuster, 2019).
121 Rohan Wilson, *Daughter of Bad Times* (Allen and Unwin, 2019) 142.
122 Bradley (n 37) 12.
123 O'Connell (n 109) 73.
124 Offill (n 89) 178.
125 Ibid.
126 Ibid 194.
127 'Season 1, Episode 4', *The Commons* (n 56) 0:38:20.
128 Ibid 0:38:07–0:38:45.
129 Ibid 0:39:03–0:39:09.
130 Alexis Wright, *The Swan Book* (Giramondo, 2013).
131 Ibid 52.
132 Ibid 31.
133 Ibid 50.
134 Ibid 58.
135 Ibid 160, 230.
136 Lydia Millet, *A Children's Bible* (WW Norton & Company, 2020).
137 Ibid 148–9.
138 Ibid 210–11.
139 Bradley (n 37) 254–9.
140 Ibid 264–5.
141 Emily St John Mandel, *Station Eleven* (Picador, 2014).
142 Cormac McCarthy, *The Road* (Picador, 2006) 157.
143 Claire Colebrook, 'The Future in the Anthropocene: Extinction and the Imagination' in Adeline Johns-Putra (ed), *Climate and Literature* (Cambridge University Press, 2019) 263, 266.
144 Adam Morton, 'Scott Morrison Pressured by Britain, France and Italy to Announce "Bold" Climate Action', *The Guardian* (online, 3 November 2020) <www.theguardian.com/australia-news/2020/nov/03/scott-morrison-pressured-by-britain-france-and-italy-to-announce-bold-climate-action>.
145 Danielle Celermajer, *Summertime: Reflections on a Vanishing Future* (Hamish Hamilton, 2021) 90.
146 Ibid 91.
147 Amy Coopes, 'Dear Australia, Elegy for a Summer of Loss', *The Guardian* (online, 23 January 2020) <www.theguardian.com/commentisfree/2020/jan/23/dear-australia-elegy-for-a-summer-of-loss>.
148 See, eg, Michael Christie, *Greenwood* (Scribe, 2019), in which 'killer dust clouds' from the 'Great Withering' lead to 'rib retch': 20–1.
149 See, eg, Marge Piercy, *Body of Glass* (Michael Joseph, 1991).
150 See, eg, *The Commons* (n 56).
151 See, eg, James Bradley, *Clade* (Hamish Hamilton, 2015); Montag (n 88); Ensor (n 120); Bertagna (n 115).

152 Lesley Head, 'Transformative Change Requires Resisting a New Normal' (2020) 10 *Nature Climate Change* 173, 174.
153 David Wallace-Wells, *An Uninhabitable Earth: A Story of the Future* (Allen Lane, 2019).
154 David Wallace-Wells, 'U.N. Climate Talks Collapsed in Madrid: What's the Way Forward?' (16 December 2019) *New York* <http://nymag.com/intelligencer/2019/12/cop25-ended-in-failure-whats-the-way-forward.html>.
155 Head (n 152) 174.
156 James Bradley, 'Terror, Hope, Anger, Kindness: The Complexity of Life as We Face the New Normal', *The Guardian* (online, 11 January 2020) <www.theguardian.com/australia-news/2020/jan/11/terror-hope-anger-kindness-the-complexity-of-life-as-we-face-the-new-normal>.
157 Jennifer Mills, 'Battling the False Narratives around Australia's Destructive Bushfires' (22 January 2020) *Literary Hub* <https://lithub.com/battling-the-false-narratives-around-australias-devastating-bushfires>.
158 Ibid.
159 Timothy Clark, *Ecocriticism on the Edge: The Anthropocene as a Threshold Concept* (Bloomsbury Publishing, 2015) 195.
160 Ibid 140.
161 Mark Mordue, 'Taste the Ash, See Our Pink Sun: Sydney's Dead Future Is Here', *The Sydney Morning Herald* (10 December 2019) <www.smh.com.au/national/taste-the-ash-see-our-pink-sun-sydney-s-dead-future-is-here-20191210-p53il4.html>.
162 Nevil Shute, *On the Beach* (Heinemann, 1957); McCarthy (n 142).
163 Eleanor Smith, 'The Poetics of Size: Rendering Apocalyptic Scale in Nevil Shute's *On the Beach* and Cormac McCarthy's *The Road*' (2018) 35/36 *Colloquy: Text, Theory, Critique* 82, 85.
164 Clark (n 159) 181.
165 Ibid 14.
166 Lucy Treloar also singles out Olivia Laing's *Crudo* and Lucy Ellmann's *Ducks, Newburyport* as examples of this: Treloar (n 43).
167 Flanagan (n 45) 21.
168 Ibid 46.
169 Ibid 94.
170 Ibid 137.
171 Ibid 103.
172 Ibid 100.
173 Ibid.
174 Leslie Jamison, 'Jenny Offill's "Weather" is Emotional, Planetary and Very Turbulent', *The New York Times* (online, 7 February 2020) <www.nytimes.com/2020/02/07/books/review/weather-jenny-offill.html>.
175 Ghosh (n 44) 54.

Index

Note: Page numbers followed by 'n' indicate a note on the corresponding page.

For Product Safety Concerns and Information please contact our EU representative GPSR@taylorandfrancis.com Taylor & Francis Verlag GmbH, Kaufingerstraße 24, 80331 München, Germany

Printed and bound by CPI Group (UK) Ltd, Croydon, CR0 4YY
14/09/2026
02216223-0007